T0311763

Cambridge Elements ≡

Elements in Politics and Communication
edited by
Stuart Soroka
University of California

BATTLEGROUND

Asymmetric Communication Ecologies and the Erosion of Civil Society in Wisconsin

Lewis A. Friedland
University of Wisconsin–Madison

Dhavan V. Shah
University of Wisconsin–Madison

Michael W. Wagner
University of Wisconsin–Madison

Chris Wells
Boston University

Katherine J. Cramer
University of Wisconsin–Madison

Jon C. W. Pevehouse
University of Wisconsin–Madison

CAMBRIDGE
UNIVERSITY PRESS

CAMBRIDGE
UNIVERSITY PRESS

University Printing House, Cambridge CB2 8BS, United Kingdom

One Liberty Plaza, 20th Floor, New York, NY 10006, USA

477 Williamstown Road, Port Melbourne, VIC 3207, Australia

314–321, 3rd Floor, Plot 3, Splendor Forum, Jasola District Centre,
New Delhi – 110025, India

103 Penang Road, #05–06/07, Visioncrest Commercial, Singapore 238467

Cambridge University Press is part of the University of Cambridge.

It furthers the University's mission by disseminating knowledge in the pursuit of
education, learning, and research at the highest international levels of excellence.

www.cambridge.org
Information on this title: www.cambridge.org/9781108925068
DOI: 10.1017/9781108946780

© Lewis A. Friedland, Dhavan V. Shah, Michael W. Wagner, Chris Wells, Katherine
J. Cramer, and Jon C. W. Pevehouse 2022

First published 2022

A catalogue record for this publication is available from the British Library.

ISBN 978-1-108-92506-8 Paperback
ISSN 2633-9897 (online)
ISSN 2633-9889 (print)

Battleground

Asymmetric Communication Ecologies and the Erosion of Civil Society in Wisconsin

Elements in Politics and Communication

DOI: 10.1017/9781108946780
First published online: January 2022

Lewis A. Friedland
University of Wisconsin–Madison

Dhavan V. Shah
University of Wisconsin–Madison

Michael W. Wagner
University of Wisconsin–Madison

Chris Wells
Boston University

Katherine J. Cramer
University of Wisconsin–Madison

Jon C. W. Pevehouse
University of Wisconsin–Madison

Author for correspondence: Lewis A. Friedland, lew.friedland@wisc.edu

Abstract: *Battleground* models Wisconsin's contentious political communication ecology: the way that politics, social life, and communication intersect and create conditions of polarization and democratic decline. Drawing from ten years of interviews, news and social media content, and statewide surveys, we combine qualitative and computational analysis with time-series and multilevel modeling to study this hybrid communication system – an approach that yields unique insights into nationalization, social structure, conventional discourses, and the lifeworld. We explore these concepts through case studies of immigration, healthcare, and economic development, concluding that despite nationalization, distinct state-level effects vary by issue as partisan actors exert their discursive power.

Keywords: Democracy, political communication, polarization, computational social science, qualitative methods

ISBNs: 9781108925068 (PB), 9781108946780 (OC)
ISSNs: 2633-9897 (online), 2633-9889 (print)

Contents

1 Introduction: Why Wisconsin?

During the decade 2010–20, the state of Wisconsin thrust itself into the national spotlight in a way that it had never done before. Wisconsin is historically a politically moderate state with a strong progressive legacy. However, in 2010 the nationwide surge of the Tea Party was felt in Wisconsin, carrying Republican Scott Walker into the governor's office. Immediately upon assuming office, Walker launched a (largely successful) frontal attack on the state's public sector unions via Act 10,[1] which brought national attention from right, left, and center. With this new national public attention, Walker made a bid for the presidency in 2016 that ultimately failed. During Walker's governorship, Wisconsin endured a blistering period of political contentiousness and division: Republicans held control of both the Assembly and Senate, but the state elected Barack Obama as president twice and split its delegation to the US Senate.

Then, in 2016, alongside Pennsylvania and Michigan, Wisconsin shocked the United States by delivering its electoral votes for Donald Trump – the first time it had favored a Republican presidential candidate since Reagan. The elections of 2018 and 2020, in which first Walker and then Trump lost Wisconsin, underscored the state's sharp political division – in the 2020 presidential election, Trump lost by about the same narrow margin (about 23,000 votes) that had delivered him the win four years earlier.

Over the same decade, our research team has been observing Wisconsin, wondering how political life here had become so contentious, so divided, and so chaotic. At the same time, we saw national-level patterns in politics and communication that clearly resembled – and sometimes seemed to follow from – what we had witnessed in Wisconsin. This similarity is produced by larger structural forces that are affecting politics at both state and national levels, and by politicians' and communicators' tendency to observe and learn from events happening elsewhere.

Clearly, state politics matter for national governance. At the national level, rural and conservative states have disproportionate power because of the structure of the Senate and the electoral college. Because these states tend to lean Republican, a very few swing states often shape the outcomes of national elections. State legislatures write laws that affect the nation as a whole: They determine who votes, when, and how long voting will take, and they legislate on criminal justice, taxation, the environment, education, and healthcare. For

---

[1] Act 10 was aimed at members of public sector labor unions. The law virtually eliminated collective bargaining rights, limited pay increases, and required union members to pay more for their benefits, effectively reducing their pay by 8 percent.

a long time, states were a backwater in the study of politics, but we have seen a resurgence of interest; recent studies have examined the balance between state and national partisanship (Hopkins, 2018), state legislative activity (Hertel-Fernandez, 2019), the rural–urban divide (Rodden, 2019), changes in federalism (Kettl, 2020), and state political ethnography (Cramer, 2016). However, there have been no systematic efforts to reconstruct state political communication ecologies: the system that binds political actors, the state and local media system, and the local communities where citizens live and form opinion.

The study of political communication within states yields critical insight into growing political partisanship, polarization, and populism. Like other scholars, we believe that political polarization is underpinned by social and civic fracture (Mason, 2018; Mason et al., 2021). These fractures cut across all levels of the polity, from the nation to the state and even to regions of states, particularly in the small-scale relations of urban and rural areas; they are embedded in local social and political life and grounded in the social network patterns that shape the lived experience of citizens. Without understanding how communication and politics interact in the states, it is difficult to assess how nationalized we really are. Wisconsin is a laboratory for the erosion of civil society at scale. As a state, it is large enough to contain every type of social and geographic unit, from large cities to sparse rural areas, but it is also sufficiently bound such that we have been able to analyze political, social, and communicative outcomes across its seventy-two counties (Dempsey et al., 2021; Suk et al., 2020; Wells et al., 2021; Witkovsky, 2021).

Wisconsin is also a continuing laboratory for understanding the conservative, populist revolt in American politics that began in 2010 (Friedland, 2020). The Tea Party-driven victories in Wisconsin were harbingers of both growing conservative control of state governments and the emergence of right-wing populism in American political life (Horwitz, 2013; Skocpol and Williamson, 2012). Wisconsin Republicans held unified control of all three branches of government from 2010 to 2018, exercising outsized political power despite having a sharply divided electorate.

Resentment of both racial minorities and state workers was central to Walker's messaging strategy, mobilizing a deep vein of "rural consciousness" that anticipated Trump's victory (Cramer, 2016). Republicans systematically rewrote the rules of the game of politics, attacking and crippling the Democratic base in public sector and teacher unions (Kaufman, 2018; Stein and Marley, 2013). Republican-controlled redistricting in 2011 led to one of the most extreme gerrymanders in the nation, cementing the "surplus power" necessary for Republicans to pursue an agenda to the right of the Wisconsin electorate

(Daley, 2016; Gilbert, 2018, 2020; Krasno et al., 2019). This eight-year experiment unleashed a decade of contention, not only in Wisconsin politics but in everyday social life. Family members and friends stopped talking to each other, sometimes for years (Wells et al., 2017), presaging the fracturing of civil society in the Trump years.

Finally, 2018 brought a Democratic resurgence, driven in part by two years of the Trump administration – and arguably, the previous eight years of right-wing state governance – leading to an almost mirror opposite presidential electoral result in 2020, with Biden winning the state by the same margin that Trump had taken it in 2016 (Gilbert, 2020).

In Wisconsin, we thus have a combination precursor, test bed, and microcosm of what was happening, and would happen, in other states as well as nationally. We ask: What factors explain the highly politically consequential shifts in Wisconsin's opinion climate over the period 2010–20? To begin answering this question, we train our lens on the state-level structures that shape discourse and contribute to forming residents' opinions. Here, we introduce the notion of *political communication ecology* – our term for the interlocked communication structures and economic, social, and political conditions that shape citizens' ideas and opinions about civic or political matters.

First, we describe the set of communication structures and participants who collaborate and compete to shape popular and official interpretations of political issues; and, second, we discuss how the dynamics of social, political, and economic conditions shape citizens' attitudes. Together, these elements provide much of the raw material on which communication processes work (i.e. the subject for interpretation). The concept of political communication ecology is a theoretical framework for interpretation and analysis across these levels.

This Element can only sketch the outlines of our findings from a decade of work. It is, however, a first step toward reconstructing these ecologies on a larger scale. We are interested in a broader, more fundamental question: How do politics, social life, media, and communication intersect to create conditions of polarization, contentiousness, and political upheaval? The study of states and regions can help us understand how national and local political forces combine with news and social media to create civic fracture. While citizens simultaneously live within nations, states, counties, and localities, communication crosscuts and overflows these boundaries. Newspapers are nested in metropolitan regions which intersect with television and radio media markets. Interpersonal networks maintain strong local ties, but social media now connects community-centered networks to state and national politics. Hyperpolarization seeps unevenly through all of these layers and networks; changes in the political economy of media industries and shifts in communication technology have substantially reshaped the dynamics of civic information networks.

Understanding these fissures – their causes and effects – is a critical first step toward combatting disinformation and rebuilding a functional polity and civil society. To understand the contemporary communication ecology, we must examine all of these layers together and study their interactions. This is a daunting task. Modern political discourse comes from many sources and directions: National elites frame issues via national media and, increasingly, social media; state political elites do the same via local newspapers, TV, and talk radio; and, in communities, citizens talk about their local schools, taxes, roads, and crime, as well as other major issues. Perhaps more difficult is the task of tracking ideas as they circulate through these different and interacting pathways: It is extremely difficult to sort out what political discourses and frames citizens encounter via particular channels. However, this is necessary if we are to understand the dynamics of civic fracture and political polarization so we can begin to address them.

Section 2 sketches our theoretical framework and offers some necessary background on Wisconsin's political communication ecology. Section 3 discusses both our broader methodological strategy of combining qualitative, survey, and computational methods and develops a map of our data and analytical procedures. Sections 4, 5, and 6 focus on case studies of three distinct issues – immigration, healthcare, and economic development, respectively – that demonstrate how political cleavages and party power vary across issues within a single state, shedding light on both nationalization and partisanship. In Section 7, we bring together the dynamics of hybrid, asymmetric communication ecologies, before concluding in Section 8 by analyzing our results and offering a roadmap for our work in the future.

2 Communication Ecologies, Social Structure, and Lifeworld

We study and understand political communication ecology through the lens of Wisconsin: the way that politics, social life, and communication media intersect, and create the current conditions of polarization, contentiousness, and political upheaval.

In recent decades, Wisconsin's communication ecology has undergone seismic shifts. State and local news, especially newspapers, which were once major institutions, have been steadily eroded by corporate decision-making and the rise of the Internet, while others, including talk radio, partisan media, and social media, have grown in prominence. These changes are altering the processes by which citizens learn about public affairs, the media in which they discuss them, the mechanisms by which campaigns contact potential supporters, and the arenas in which public debates take place. And although our analysis is through a Wisconsin context, similar transformations are occurring across the United States, and indeed around the world. Mapping these processes systematically and in their interrelationships, we argue, is an urgent task for scholars who wish to understand the rapidly changing contexts of political communication.

This Element takes a first step toward this goal by mapping these relations in a single state. We begin in this section by developing our theory of the *political communication ecology*, which encompasses three major elements and their interrelations: the *communication ecology*, made up of the institutions and spaces that foster communication, from the intimacy of interpersonal friend and familial networks to the breadth of news and social media; the *political system*, including parties, elites, and partisanship; and the layer of *social life* that structures community social networks and citizens' everyday experiences in the lifeworld. In what follows, we briefly describe these three components before delving more deeply into the political communication ecology they constitute.

The changing structure of the media system is the subject of ongoing examination within communication research (e.g. Chadwick 2017; Williams and Delli Carpini, 2011). This broader theoretical interest in the changing nature of media systems has shaped our communication ecological framework. We attend closely to the contributions of a variety of actors – from journalists, editors, and news-making elites to citizens and activists in social media – and describe layers of flow and interdependence among these communicators. And we examine which communicators, under what conditions, have the capacity to shape public discourse and understanding. We ask the same questions others are asking, but aim to answer them in a more expansive way, accounting for a wider set of relationships and interactions: specifically, between the changing communication ecology and the political and social contexts in which it sits. This more capacious, more integrative perspective is currently only manageable at the level of the single state. We hope to inspire others to do the same in other states and in national regions to build a framework for comparison.

The communication ecology is linked to the political system across a number of axes. One central theme in this Element addresses the growing debate over the nationalization of politics (Hopkins, 2018), testing whether the political orientations of elites and citizens are indeed (as the received wisdom has it) shaped from the top down, springing primarily from elite partisan divisions at a national level and flowing downward through state elites, then onward to activists, and finally trickling down to less politically engaged citizens in their everyday lives. We ask: How well does this pattern hold in the case of a single state, and how does it vary at the state level, both within and across issues?

A second central political theme is party asymmetry – the claim that the two major parties now operate via different democratic and political norms, elite networks, and media ecologies. Most studies of asymmetry have focused on elites and media ecologies at the national level. Here, we advance research in the field by focusing at a more granular level, showing more precisely how political discourses and frames flow across political, communication, and social layers. Our findings support the claim by Benkler et al. (2018) and others that the discourses, which shape everyday political life, reflect the different strategies Republican (symbolic) and Democratic (policy-oriented) elites use when framing issues (Wagner and Gruszczynski, 2016). We incorporate the concept of discursive power, developed by Jungherr et al. (2019), which connects flows of influence and power within and across media systems, but again, we show that there is variation by issue and social location.

The third key political theme of this Element is the effect of social life on political opinion. Political communication analysis has generally not taken account of social life beyond the social and demographic characteristics of individuals. We take two steps in this direction. First, we analyze the socio-geographic and social-structural context that shapes places – regions, communities, neighborhoods (Suk et al., 2020) – as well as social networks (Friedland, 2016), using both qualitative and multilevel analysis. Second, we (re)introduce the concept of the lifeworld to political communication, the everyday experiences that anchor people's place in social life and through which they interpret political and social experience and shape the issue positions that circulate as conventional discourses (Strauss, 2012). Here, we develop an operational framework that incorporates both social-structural and lifeworld perspectives and links them to the communication ecology at local, regional, and state levels.

2.1 Communication Ecology, Media Systems, and Discursive Power

Our theory of a communication ecology is rooted in the assumption that public discussions of political issues, and related public opinions and behaviors, are shaped by the structure and dynamics of the *systems* in which they take place. Such a systems perspective has become increasingly prevalent in the last twenty years, as the digital revolution has diversified and proliferated media forms. Chadwick's (2017) "hybrid media system" is the point of reference for twenty-first century communication scholars thinking of the media space as a system. Chadwick articulated the hybridity of political communication systems, which are neither yet fully "digital" nor any longer defined by the broadcast logics of the twentieth century. His analyses highlighted the growing potential influence of new entrants to political discourse, from networks of bloggers to citizens armed with the capacities of social media; they also articulated the challenges faced by the political parties and news organizations of the *ancien régime* that struggle to find their footing in the new environment. The movement toward systems thinking in our field has increased our attention to the complexity of contemporary communication environments, which are constituted by: (a) diverse entities (individuals, institutions) with diverse and often conflicting objectives; (b) at multiple levels; (c) interacting with, and in response to, one another; and (d) often producing emergent and nonlinear effects (Page, 2010; Shah et al., 2017).

Central to systems thinking is the question of how power is manifested. To clarify the nature of power within communication systems, Jungherr and colleagues (2019), building on Chadwick's framework, have introduced the notion of "discursive power." Actors can be said to exercise discursive power when they "introduce, amplify, and maintain topics, frames, and speakers that other contributors" then pick up, use, and adopt (p. 409). In other words, the capacity to shape others' interpretations, understandings, and descriptions of political phenomena is a form of political power that operates through communication (Castells, 2007).

Benkler and colleagues (2018) have offered one of the most concretely empirical descriptions of how such power operates within the US national-level political media system. In the context of the 2016 presidential election, they reveal how key actors, located at a variety of points in the system, and working across multiple platforms and modes of media creation (including an array of legacy news organizations and digital-born newcomers), shaped the discourse and news agenda surrounding the candidates. Structurally, they demonstrate that the US political communication system is bifurcated asymmetrically; by 2016, a cluster of strongly right-leaning media (centered on *Breitbart* and *Fox News*) had cleaved off from centrist conventional news, creating a subsystem of its own, while left-leaning media remained strongly tied to centrist news sources. Benkler et al. (2018) present evidence for multiple flows of influence within the larger media system, sometimes in unexpected directions – such as *Breitbart's* apparent influence on mainstream outlets' treatment of information harmful to Hillary Clinton. In Jungherr's (2019) terms, this was a clear exercise of discursive power by the far right, as one set of actors succeeded in setting, to some degree, the terms of the national debate about a key political figure.

2.1.1 The Hybrid Media System: National and Local

The accounts cited above, however, are centered on *national* hybrid media systems, and they focus primarily on the interactions between journalism and elite political opinion. Our approach to political communication ecology develops and extends these approaches in two ways. First, we stress that the communication ecology is multilayered: Moving vertically, we can identify layers from the national media systems to those in states (in the American context), metro regions, local communities, and neighborhoods, including interpersonal networks and microinteractions. Second, we trace the horizontal communication flows that function differently within each layer, connecting individuals, groups, and networks via news frames and narratives (Friedland, 2001). Given the political and perceptual significance of place (e.g. Cramer, 2016), we suspected that the statewide political communication ecology would be the level at which we could most fruitfully observe the interactions among news media, citizen talk, and individual experience.

The exchanges in the national system have been primarily among political, cultural, and economic elites and the journalists who cover them, setting the boundaries of national or intraparty consensus (Bennett, 2011). We trace a similar set of interchanges that take place at the state, metro, and local levels, with the difference that a broader range of social and community actors has to be taken into account (state and local government, community leaders, citizens) (Anderson, 2013; Kaniss, 1991; Robinson, 2017). We also describe this dynamic as it emerges within communities and neighborhoods, where a rich horizontal flow of communication takes up elite opinion, recognizes what is relevant, circulates it, and translates it into everyday concerns (Friedland, 2014; Matsaganis et al., 2010; Shah et al., 2001).

In this Element, our primary goal is to advance a *theory of political communication ecology*. To illustrate this theory, we apply it to communication about politics in Wisconsin from 2016 through 2018 with the goal of demonstrating how a hybrid political communication ecology works at federal, regional, and local levels. We analytically describe the entities (individuals and groups in communities, as well as parties and their partisan supporters) with diverse political objectives (power, influence, and persuasion) at multiple levels (nation, state, metro-region, and community). We chart and analyze some of these entities' interactions and the flows that pass among them, which cut across multiple media and communication modes (mass, social, interpersonal). We identify emergent effects where we can. But by focusing on the large but bounded domain of a single state, our analysis both demonstrates and points toward even more complex interactions and serves as a preliminary sketch for a more complete and systematic future analysis.

2.1.2 The Political Communication Ecology at the State Level

There are several reasons for attending to communication ecologies at the state level. For one, states continue to exercise formidable political power in critical areas of policymaking, from the regulation of voting and the creation of legislative districts to taxation, education, and criminal justice. Furthermore, discourses developing at state levels can test, mediate, and modify the discourses at play nationally.

Investigating a communication ecology at the state level also allows us to attend more closely to the dynamics of citizens' social lives and media experiences. Historically, American news attention has been strongly locally rooted, and local news continues to make up a central aspect of the average citizen's news diet (Wells et al., 2021). Even after years of local news decline and the increasing nationalization of news coverage, more American households receive a city or state-oriented newspaper than a national one (Barthel, 2019). News outlets have historically been oriented to local concerns (at the level of a city, metro area, or county), with most newspapers explicitly tied to a locale and American broadcast television rooted in local stations, which affiliate with national networks (Usher, 2019).

2.1.3 Nationalization of Politics

We can best explain the nature of statewide communication ecologies by beginning at the familiar level of national political discourse and working down. At the widest angle, states and their media ecologies are interpenetrated with national-level events and national media systems. In the US federated republic, this has always been the case, but nationalization is increasing, and what happens in lower levels of politics more and more closely mirrors dynamics at the federal level. Hopkins (2018) has argued that state and national voting patterns are increasingly aligned with national and state identities, rendering sociogeographic and regional differences almost irrelevant: "[O]nce we know the basic demographic facts about an individual, knowing her place of residence adds little to our understanding of a variety of political attitudes" (p. 14).

However, nationalization bears more fine-grained analysis, as the process is incomplete and unevenly distributed sociogeographically. Just as the United States is divided between more urban and more rural states, each type increasingly dominated by a single party, this pattern is reproduced in state subregions and counties. What is presented as a divide is more of a patterned distribution of concentric circles (Badger et al., 2021; Rodden, 2019; Wells et al., 2021). Even towns of a few thousand are more Democratic than their surrounds. Small cities and their suburbs are critical swing areas precisely because they don't always neatly reproduce rural or urban patterns.

Nationalization increases the importance of the local information environment by connecting it to state (and, in turn, national) politics. But, paradoxically, nationalization also helps to destroy these local environments. As Hopkins shows, there has been a long-term shift from local news sources (newspapers and local television) to national sources, caused by a primary shift in the *types* of media consumed (from mass to social, and broadcast to cable). According to Hopkins (2018), this shift to cable and online news sources is leaving behind "the sources of what little state and local information we do receive" (p. 212).

If most studies of the American media system focus on the national level, it is because nation-oriented media shape state-level media systems (see, e.g., Benkler et al., 2018). We certainly agree that the major concerns and trends of the national communication ecology reach consumers both directly, as they watch national network news, and indirectly, as nationally defined issues are addressed and interpreted by more local media and within social networks. However, as this Element shows, this is not the whole story: we find much greater variation in the communication ecology at the state level than this account would lead us to expect.

2.2 State and Local News in Wisconsin

State news coverage is dependent on how much state news is reported in local television and newspapers, but local news coverage in Wisconsin, as across the United States, is in linear decline. An unsustainable business model has led to massive ownership consolidation. Shrinking revenue drives radical staff cuts, resulting in "zombie" news organizations and "news deserts" (Abernathy, 2018; Barthel, 2019; Napoli, 2018). What state coverage breaks through to the wider public is determined, in part, by this "last mile" of local news, which is in crisis.

Our analysis of news consumption patterns across Wisconsin (Wells et al., 2021) demonstrated that mainstream media still play a central role in people's *news* experience. Television and local newspapers consistently outrank internet and social media use in every geographic area. Local television is still the modal source of news for respondents in virtually every part of the state, with the suburbs of smaller cities showing significantly higher local TV news viewing than other areas. Local TV news has larger audiences than local newspapers (though newspapers still provide the bulk of the original reporting that underpins all local and state news). While local TV viewership may be in secular decline and its audience may skew older, it remains crucial to political communication at the local and state level (Mitchell and Matsa, 2019). Local news shapes both the ways citizens *imagine* local communities and the lens through which they understand all issues: national, state, and local.

Yet we also found that even the peak of local television news use represents only *occasional* news consumption, declining to *rare* consumption for any social media news. In sum, we found that *most people do not pay much attention to news most of the time, via any medium.* It is easy to lose sight of this, given the intense scholarly focus on how news moves via social media. High news attenders (who tend to be more partisan) make up a small proportion of the total audience. Most people's *news* media diets still resemble the patterns of a decade or even two decades ago; some simply supplement that news diet with news distributed by Facebook, which also serves as a social network connector (Guess et al., 2018; Prior, 2007).

2.2.1 Local Television

Since local television is the modal source of news, its patterns of ownership, production, and political coverage are central to the flow of state news as a whole. The content of local television news varies with tradition and ownership. Wisconsin has seven major television markets (in outline in Figure 1), some owned by small groups that invest more than the norm in local coverage. However, when stations are bought out by larger groups, the cycle of disinvestment and dilution begins. Disinvestment reduces local reporting, but producers must maintain or expand total hours on-air. This dilutes the ratio of reporting to airtime and favors national news over local, since affiliate feeds can be used at marginal cost to fill time. It also further favors local over state coverage, since much of the local news slot can be filled relatively cheaply with episodic content. This cycle leaves state and local political coverage to wither.

Several stations in Madison remain state news powerhouses that feed regional affiliates, supporting the claim that state capitals receive a higher quantity and quality of state news, in part due to their political geography (Delli Carpini, 1996). The map of Wisconsin counties and large metros with news designated market areas (DMAs) provides some sense of these differences (see Figure 1). Similarly, several Milwaukee stations employ experienced Capitol correspondents. However, ownership matters: Sinclair Broadcasting, which has increasingly slanted its coverage to favor right-wing views and politicians, now owns five stations in the top three Wisconsin cities (although only Green Bay is a major VHF station). According to recent studies, an increase in local Sinclair ownership led to: (a) a substantial increase of national coverage at the expense of local politics; (b) a rightward ideological shift; and (c) a decrease in viewership (Levendusky, 2021; Martin and McCrain, 2019).

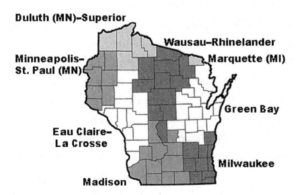

Figure 1 Wisconsin counties and large metros with news DMAs

These findings are consistent with trends toward nationalization and polarization, which have negative implications for local coverage and accountability.
In Wisconsin's particular political ecology, these changes in the communication system have asymmetric partisan consequences, as the Republican Party of
Wisconsin has recognized and taken strategic advantage of the continuing
power of local television news. For example, starting in 2011, Governor
Walker flew from city to city in the state plane, offering sound bites or live
shots in the critical 4–6 p.m. news slot, but leaving no time for follow-up
questions from newspaper reporters (interview with Brian Reisinger, 2017).
We have no direct measurement of the effects of this strategy, but his savvy
veteran campaign team believed it was very effective.

2.2.2 Local Newspapers

Newspapers remain the most comprehensively local and civic of media, anchoring citizens in verified, complex information about their everyday lives in their
specific sociogeography. Most Wisconsin towns of reasonable size had newspapers with active local reporting well into the last decades of the twentieth
century, and many still do. But newspapers in Wisconsin, as elsewhere, are
under great stress (Althaus et al., 2009; Hayes and Lawless, 2017; Nielsen,
2015). Despite the rise of national alternative media (and the nonprofit local and
regional news now published online [Kim et al., 2016; Konieczna, 2018; Usher,
2017]), no sustainable online sources have arisen to replace newspapers, which
remain the anchor of fact-based discourse in local and state ecologies.

In the 2000s, Wisconsin newspapers began to be radically consolidated, and
papers shrank in reporting staff, circulation, and influence. The Gannett news
group, the largest group in the United States, has purchased independent mid-
sized papers in critical swing cities of the so-called "BOW" counties: Green
Bay, Oshkosh, and Appleton, as well as Wausau, Sheboygan, and Manitowoc. It
crowned its consolidation with the purchase of the state flagship *Milwaukee
Journal Sentinel* in 2016. This consolidation under Gannett has left the state
vulnerable to the potential collapse of the newspaper layer of the communication ecology as a functioning civic information source. The successful 2019
acquisition of Gannett by Gatehouse media (summarized in a *New York Times*
headline as "Hedge fund called 'Destroyer of Newspapers' bids for USA Today
owner Gannett") is accelerating the hollowing out of Wisconsin's newspaper
ecology (although the level of reporting at its flagship remains high).

As a consequence of this consolidation, Wisconsin has seen the emergence of
"zombie newspapers": Staff cuts shrink local and state coverage, while the
papers are kept alive to milk local advertising revenue. Gannett habitually cuts

newsroom staff and consolidates multiple papers into single "bureaus," often leaving cities previously covered by scores of reporters with no more than five staff. In Wisconsin, this is particularly true in medium-sized cities that are the swing determiners of statewide political contests. A semiretired business owner in the Fox Valley (the critical BOW counties) who has read the daily local paper for years laments, "Now they have no local stuff. It's a regional paper."

This decline of newspaper quantity and quality has led to a severe drop in reporting about the state. In the 1990s, there were regularly twenty to thirty local and regional reporters in the Capitol. In 1999–2000 there were fourteen full-time newspaper reporters covering the Capitol; by 2020, there were only eight, plus some news services and public radio. The broad effect of cutting back statehouse reporting is straightforward: less state-level news is supplied to the state as a whole as well as to specific regions and cities. But a second, barely studied problem, is the vanishing coverage of *locally relevant state news*, particularly coverage of local state Assembly and Senate delegations. In 1985, the then independently owned *Racine Journal Times*, serving a county of about 170,000 residents, had its own statehouse correspondent who covered both the Racine and Kenosha delegations. Today, only the largest metro papers regularly cover local state legislative delegations (interview with Peter Fox, 2020). There is precious little daily or weekly journalism on these delegations' policy positions, voting patterns, and contributors. This collapse is a critical and understudied ecosystem failure in the statewide news niche – one that is almost certainly happening in other states with similar communications ecosystems.

2.2.3 Statewide Media

There are several additional sources of statewide news that partly fill the gap left by declining newspaper coverage. First is *Wisconsin Public Radio* (WPR), the state's 100-year-old statewide radio network. WPR is arguably the only mainstream news counterpart to the right-wing talk radio that saturates the state's radio waves (see Section 2.2.4). The WPR talk network has strong ratings throughout the state; about 75 percent of its audience is in Madison, Milwaukee, Green Bay, and Appleton, but it also posts strong audience numbers in outstate cities. It may also serve as a crossover medium; some callers regularly cite Rush Limbaugh or Sean Hannity on WPR news-talk programs (interview with Dean Kallenbach, 2020). In many places, WPR is the primary provider of state political and public affairs coverage.

A second influential source of statewide news is the Wisconsin Center for Investigative Journalism (WCIJ). Founded in 2009, WCIJ engages in critical, investigative, nonpartisan reporting on a wide range of state issues. The content it produces can be republished for free; WCIJ stories therefore run in more than 150 news outlets across the state (often on the front pages of newspapers) and are disseminated via a partnership with WPR. It is hard to directly estimate the effect of WCIJ reporting, since much of it is carried by other news organizations. Nevertheless, even the strongest statewide nonprofits like WCIJ cannot substitute for missing coverage of local state delegations.

A third source of state news is independent reporting from partisan media. The right has long funded state reporting networks. Millions of dollars from the Bradley Foundation support the Badger Report and MacIver Institute, and the Franklin News Foundation funded the *Wisconsin Reporter* until 2017. To counterbalance this, the *Wisconsin Examiner* was launched in 2019 as part of the State Newsroom network, a group of left-leaning news outlets (Spicuzza and Marley, 2019). Although there is little evidence of the independent effect of these partisan sources on mainstream reporting, the conservative outlets' connection to talk radio and their presence on Twitter and other social networks (Section 2.3) likely increases the overall circulation of right-wing ideas and frames.

2.2.4 Conservative Talk Radio

It is well established that in the conservative communication ecosystem national talk radio has played a key role in opinion formation at the national level (Jamieson and Cappella, 2008). Since the 1990s, talk radio has also played an understudied role in state and local opinion formation in two ways.

First, conservative talk radio *anchors* the national ultraconservative political and ideological environment within the states, and this ties voters to the Republican Party on both national and state issues by providing a dedicated state-local conservative audience with a constant stream of partisan political content. In Wisconsin, twenty-six radio stations are "news-talk," almost all carrying ultraconservative programs. In 2016, Hannity and Limbaugh were carried by thirteen and twelve stations respectively, an average of three hours each per day, followed with other national hosts filling most of the broadcast day.

Second, Wisconsin has its own state-specific talk radio ecology, and national saturation alone understates conservative talk influence in Wisconsin. Since the 1980s, two Milwaukee AM 50,000 watt powerhouse stations have blanketed Wisconsin with near nonstop conservative talk radio content. The majority of this content, which dominates the airwaves, both in terms of hours and station carriage, has come from three state talkers: Charlie Sykes (who retired in 2016 and was replaced by a sitting ultraconservative Republican assemblyman),

Mark Belling, and Vicki McKenna. These three have focused on Wisconsin issues and politics and created state-focused conservative talk radio ecologies that are among the most powerful in the nation.

Sykes was the best known and most influential of the three. He was instrumental in Scott Walker's surprise election to the Milwaukee County Executive in 2002 and promoted both of Walker's runs for governor (the unsuccessful 2006 campaign and the successful 2010 run). During his governorship, Walker continued to regularly appear on Sykes' show, testing and promoting campaign themes (interview with Charlie Sykes, 2017). Perhaps most importantly, though, Sykes (who became a never-Trumper and retired from his show in 2016) enforced conservative discipline in what was then a broader Republican Party, shaping the national and state conversations and state party.

Wisconsin's talk radio ecology also includes many *local talk radio* shows. While local shows receive much less scholarly attention than nationally syndicated and statewide shows, they are important to the overall political communication ecology of states; they contextualize national and international issues, translating them into local terms by trusted local voices, and they provide information about local elections and political events, mobilizing listeners. In addition, they often host national candidates or their surrogates. For example, in the 2020 election cycle, local Wisconsin talk shows hosted national Trump surrogates, including Eric Trump and Tennessee Republican Senator Marsha Blackburn (Cramer, forthcoming).

2.3 Social Media

Capturing the role of social media at the state level poses particular challenges. Every social media platform spans all layers of the communication ecology, from national to local to interpersonal. Furthermore, each platform is used by somewhat different but overlapping audiences and performs different functions.

Twitter is the medium that we have analyzed most intensively. It clearly forms a distinct national communication layer that connects elites, journalists, and educated, attentive citizens, who tend to be more partisan than average. Twitter itself is an integral part of the national social media ecology (Benkler et al., 2018), shaping the flow of news discourse both *horizontally* within the national layer but also *vertically* downward to reach a similar grouping of elites in the states. These state elites (e.g. local legislators, media professionals, party operatives, and advocacy organizations that are connected to the national elites and state citizens via Twitter) shape, transmit, and interpret this national discourse, modifying and applying it to state issues and groups using state-level conventional discourses and frames (see Section 3). This state layer also connects social media news users to other mass and niche media outlets *within* the state; for instance, when citizens follow local or regional newspapers to share headlines.

However, it is difficult to precisely ascertain the role of Twitter in state-level discourse, because many end-users can and do skip the state level of mediation altogether. Trump, for example, directly communicated with his followers without the mediation of state elites. This means that some national-level discourses and frames reach mass social media audiences in the states directly while others are sifted and reshaped by state actors, and it is difficult to parse the effect of each, since they circularly reinforce each other. As a social media network, Twitter connects users to more or less horizontal and heterogeneous social media networks which recirculate both national and state frames alongside personal narratives in the lifeworld.

However, Twitter does not reach everyone. Twitter users tend to be more politically engaged and more partisan than users of other social media platforms and even more so when compared with people who do not consume news via social media at all. Different social media platforms appeal to different groups and have different functions for those groups. Google's YouTube, used by 81 percent of Americans, feeds news and partisan content, driven by everyday search functions and YouTube's audience engagement algorithm. Facebook, the second most used platform (69 percent), connects across multiple dimensions of social life; it is most directly anchored in the everyday lifeworld of its users (Shearer and Mitchell, 2021), and therefore shares news and political content through more heavily used personal networks, gaining the persuasive power of recommendation. Because of this network anchoring, Facebook may play a stronger role in the intersecting circulation of personal and local-state narratives. Thorson et al. (2020) have argued that Facebook is increasingly displacing traditional local media in the civic sphere, but this remains the largest gap in our research. We are currently studying the ways in which county party Facebook pages contributed to the discourse surrounding election fraud in 2020. Preliminary results indicate that local Republican Party Facebook pages played a large role in amplifying election fraud claims that originated with national conservative elites and right-wing news media, publicizing these claims and translating them for local audiences.

2.4 Lifeworld, Conventional Discourses, and Social Structure

The breadth and complexity of contemporary communication ecologies – not to mention the *political* communication ecologies of which they are part – pose a daunting challenge for analysts. To make that complexity manageable, we have developed a working model of the full political communication ecology that articulates relationships among key communication media and interpersonal networks at several levels of specificity. In this section, we present that model before elaborating our notions of lifeworld, conventional discourses, and social structure, and showing how they interact with the communication ecology.

Our model (see Figure 2) centers the citizen in a lifeworld of everyday experience that is shaped by a physical reality – place – that structures social life and is populated by individuals with whom that person has interpersonal, face-to-face interactions. Although we do not depict it in the figure, this lifeworld is very much the product of a person's location within a wider social-structural matrix of class, race, gender, and geography. The importance of these factors is apparent in the results from our regression models in Sections 4, 5, and 6, where the lion's share of variance is explained by demographic variables.

A person's social networks are largely coextensive with – in fact, partly constitutive of – their lifeworld; but social networks, to varying degrees, also extend beyond an individual's particular lifeworld. Members of our social networks convey exposure to other experiences and opinions –they are channels through which the patterned habits of thinking about and discussing political issues, which Strauss (2012) has termed "conventional discourses," flow. For these reasons, our analyses underscore the centrality of interpersonal talk to political opinion formation, and we conceive and operationalize the concept

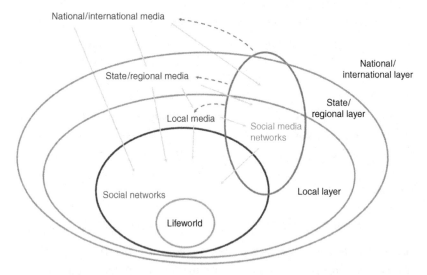

Figure 2 Model of a political communication ecology

"conventional discourses" as always embedded within the context of interpersonal networks.

However, those conventional discourses are not somehow walled off from the presentations of political events that are disseminated by professionalized media (Polletta and Callahan, 2017). Figure 2 depicts several of the ways in which locality, personal networks, and media intersect. First, we make clear that there are media – here, we primarily have in mind news media – that are oriented to audiences at national, state, and local levels; the information presented by these media may reach an individual directly, through consumption choices, or indirectly, through the mediation of a social network (such as a conversation partner or network-connected other who listens to talk radio and adopts its conventional discourses).

Second, we depict social media as having both a particular relationship to a person's network and as serving a number of communicative roles. We show that social media networks are an amalgam of network connections from varying levels of proximity. As we have pointed out elsewhere (Wells et al., 2021), the field needs better measures of the makeup of social media networks; however, the available data strongly suggest that, for most individuals, these networks are dominated by contacts that, at some time, have shared a physical locality with the individual, such as neighbors or high school contacts who now live in another town or state (Hampton, 2016). We represent this visually by presenting the social media "space" as spanning several levels of proximity while remaining strongly rooted in the "local" layer.

Finally, Figure 2 shows that social media can serve as a channel that runs in both directions: it not only transports information and discourses from news media to citizens but also transmits citizens' social media discourses back to news media. The latter occurs both in the sense of direct interactions among citizens, activists, political elites, and journalists and via aggregate measures of audience interest and attention (see, e.g., McGregor, 2019). In either case, as our analyses imply, there is potential bidirectional influence in terms of the depictions of political issues. However, there is as yet no solid information comparing how much news content at the local, state, and national levels circulates in social media, and this important question should be empirically investigated.

2.4.1 The Lifeworld

The immediate experiences that shape citizens' views can be captured through the concept of the *lifeworld*, which builds on the insight that all social actors live in "worlds of everyday experience" that constitute their primary realities and make mutual understanding possible (Schutz and Luckmann, 1973, p. 35).[2] These worlds are irreducibly social and cultural and are deeply anchored in place (Friedland, 2016): Social actors live in neighborhoods surrounded by people like themselves on most but not all dimensions. Our social networks are built from these local places, including those groups that constitute our social identities, beginning with primary socialization in the family and secondary socialization with peers, and continuing throughout our life-courses in our everyday encounters and experiences with others.

Interpersonal political talk – the many informal conversations citizens have with one another as they make sense of political topics – arises from and primarily exists at the level of the lifeworld. A wealth of research has detailed the significance of political talk in helping citizens to anchor and organize their understandings of the political world (Cramer, 2004, 2007; Huckfeldt and Sprague, 1995; Shah et al., 2005). The lifeworld is a critical site for the development and distribution of Hochschild's (2016) "deep stories" – narratives that (like Cramer's [2016] "rural consciousness") bind people together in identity groups and shape their experience of the world, and the boundaries between self and other. Such narratives are rarely invoked explicitly and fully, either in memory or in conversation, but they are the lens through which we interpret events.

In a communication ecological framework, lifeworlds provide the critical ground floor at which citizens reconcile the material reality of their lives (the job they do, the storefronts they see in their community, the lives of their friends and families) with interpretations of politics circulating in media and conversation. Importantly, as Couldry and Hepp (2016) have shown, the lifeworld itself is transforming as communicatively mediated experience occupies a wider and wider portion of citizens' attention. While we generally accept that this shift is occurring, we do not presuppose that social media have yet fully or even primarily overridden the socially constructed components of the lifeworld that are analytically prior to mediated experience – family socialization and peer interactions. This analytic separation allows us to hold the primacy of the effects of the communication ecology on public opinion as an empirical question.

---

[2] Schutz's concept of the lifeworld is limited to the world of everyday action and experience. Habermas (1987) uses it much more broadly, signifying the complex of culture, society, and personality that anchors communicative action, distinguishing it from the systems of money and power. Our use here is in the more restrictive Schutzian sense, although the relation of lifeworld to social systems could be more systematically explicated in the context of our cases, which we hope to do in the future (Friedland, 2001).

2.4.2 Conventional Discourses

As the empirical sections of this Element demonstrate, we have found the framework of *conventional discourses* (Strauss, 2012) to be a powerful way to think about how public opinion is created. Citizens' opinions are not only the product of objective experienced conditions, nor are they invented out of whole cloth by depictions in the media. Rather, our communication ecological framework posits that opinion occurs at the intersection of these two: at the place where propositions, expressed discursively, credibly depict the reality that citizens encounter in their lifeworlds. Opinion is created in mediated communication, in interpersonal political talk, and within citizens' own experience and mind.

As Strauss, citing Bakhtin (1981), notes, our everyday opinions are "half-ours and half someone else's" (Strauss, 2012, p. 15). Many of our words and ideas come from members of our *opinion community,* including our social networks and, increasingly, our shared memberships in audiences and social media networks. We also learn and use the essential ingredients of conventional discourses – their metaphors, comparisons, assertions – that circulate through multiple forms of communication. As Strauss emphasizes, these discourses are exchanged in interpersonal settings. But, as Polletta and Callahan (2017) show, social conversation anchored by deep stories combines ecologically with news consumption and social media sharing to form a complex whole. We know that people's media diets and repertoires shape opinion outcomes (Edgerly, 2015; Thorson and Wells, 2015). We understand how elites set opinion agendas, and we know that social media (particularly Twitter) allows elites to both affect and be affected by news (Neuman et al., 2014; Wells et al., 2016; Gruszczynski and Wagner, 2017; Posegga and Jungherr, 2019). In this Element, we explore how the interaction of elite-generated opinion (including at the state level) and media repertoires set the parameters for the opinion environments of people in their everyday worlds.

2.4.3 Social-Structural Context

The lifeworld experiences of citizens are obviously not arbitrarily or randomly distributed through society: lifeworlds are patterned by larger social structures, including economic, occupational, racial, geographic, and partisan differences. However, these two dimensions – lifeworld and social structure – are analytically separate: The structuring of social life and networks creates the context within which lifeworld communication occurs.

Here, our understanding of social structure incorporates both the systems (political, economic, social) that organize society and the ways they impact individuals' and social groups' everyday experiences – their lifeworlds. In the United States, the overarching political-economic systems are organized into a federal structure, and they progressively narrow and become more specific as they move downward through states, state subregions, counties, local communities, neighborhoods, and social groups. The communication system parallels this structure: national media continue to set the dominant agendas and frames of debate; and state politics and media communicate and translate national-level issues downward to the local level (and, to a limited degree, local-level issues upward). Local communication is closer to everyday experience and understood as most relevant (Friedland, 2001).

Citizens' communicative experiences are, of course, shaped by their location in the social structure – their class, occupation, education, age, ethnicity, race, and gender. But these are not independent variables. They cluster in social networks that are more or less homophilous, connecting people who are similar in socially meaningful ways; these networks and their members are shaped by the geographically structured social space of neighborhoods and communities (Centola, 2015; McPherson et al., 2001; Ognyanova, 2019)

2.4.4 Wisconsin's Changing Social Structure

In this section, we describe key elements of Wisconsin's social structure, and three broad social–economic transformations that have taken place in recent decades. Those changes create the context for the specific case explorations that constitute the empirical sections of the Element: the economy, race and immigration, and growing division between rural and urban areas.

Economic transformation. In the period after World War II, Wisconsin's economy was anchored in manufacturing and farming. In 2002, the state was still unionized well above the national average (18.7 percent vs.14.9 percent, respectively), and labor strength was relatively broadly distributed throughout urban and rural areas. However, the 1980s saw the start of a secular decline in high-paying industrial union jobs, a slow weakening of unions, and a rise in economic inequality throughout the upper Midwest (Rodrik, 2016). During the deindustrialization process, labor strength shifted away from manufacturing unions to service and teacher unions. Yet, in 2011, teacher unions were abolished in Wisconsin under Act 10, which attacked public sector unions on the pretext of addressing a projected budget deficit, and a "right-to-work" law followed in 2015.

Wisconsin still has the second highest percentage of the workforce employed in manufacturing (including food processing) nationally at just under 16 percent, but after the passage of Act 10 and right-to-work, union membership in

Wisconsin abruptly dropped below the national average; by 2018, only 8.6 percent of Wisconsin labor was unionized, compared to 11.7 percent of workers at the national level. By 2018, levels of state inequality were higher than they had been in 100 years (Dresser and Rogers, 2019). Because of the combination of rising inequality and deunionization, working-class Wisconsinites have seen their standards of living decline substantially since the 1980s.

Race and Immigration. Union decline destroyed an important bridge between white workers and workers of color and added further fuel to the politics of racial resentment. The deindustrialization of the 1980s had particularly disastrous and unequal consequences for African-Americans. Rising poverty allowed Republican political discourse to stigmatize Milwaukee as a "welfare basket case" and its residents as parasites on "hard-working" (white) Wisconsinites. This became the central organizing trope of Republican politics more generally: Wisconsin Republicans made appeals to hard-working, (implicitly) white working- and middle-class families, particularly in suburban and rural areas, by framing their declining standards of living as caused by exploitation at the hands of a class of "takers": African-Americans in Milwaukee, state employees in Madison, and teachers and public sector workers throughout the state.

Racial politics have also changed as more and more Latinos moved to Wisconsin and out of areas where they had historically been concentrated – in the Milwaukee and southeast working class. During the 2000s, immigrant groups diffused throughout Wisconsin. The number of hired workers in dairy (in rural areas) nearly doubled from 2006–17 (Hall and Vetterkind, 2017); many of these workers are Latino, some documented and some undocumented. Nationally, Republican rhetoric is anti-immigration, and particularly anti-undocumented workers, who are framed as "stealing Americans' jobs." However, in Wisconsin, dairy farmers now depend on this labor to keep their farms alive. As we will see in Section 4, attitudes toward immigration in Wisconsin, even among Republicans and Trump voters, are more complex than the national Republican symbolic framing would predict, and they are mediated by these social-structural and lifeworld factors.

Rural Consciousness. Cramer (2016) has identified an underlying rural consciousness among white Wisconsinites consisting of three core beliefs: rural areas do not get their fair share of decision-making power; rural people work harder, have "better values," and are distinct in their lifestyle and culture from urban residents; and rural areas are being deprived of their fair share of resources by cities, whose residents condescend toward rural residents. Nonetheless, in Wisconsin, as elsewhere, tax dollars flow from urban to rural areas, and rural areas are overrepresented in the Wisconsin legislature both because of the distribution of partisan voters (Chen and Rodden, 2013) and extreme gerrymandering (Daley, 2016; Krasno et al., 2019).)

Yet these perceptions of rural disadvantage are not completely unfounded. They are grounded in a set of real, interlocking problems: rural underemployment, population decline, and farm crisis. Rural economies in Wisconsin have been in decline since at least the early 1980s, and, by 2018, Wisconsin led the United States in farm bankruptcies. As farms go under, town economies suffer as well (Barrett, 2019). With federal and state cutbacks removing economic safety nets, local rural governments have had to assume greater responsibility for public services of all kinds. These include schools – important anchors of community identity that are becoming more difficult to sustain.

Rural demographics are also changing: When young people leave (to go to college or to seek work elsewhere), they are unlikely to return. This contributes to the graying of the rural population, which in turn increases demand for caregiving and the need for healthcare. In many rural areas, the hospital, usually in the county seat, has replaced the farm or the factory as the most important source of quality employment, particularly for women. Yet the state legislature refuses to accept federal Medicaid funding, thus giving the issue of healthcare a particular resonance in the everyday lives of all Wisconsinites.

These trends – youth flight, farm decline, and population aging – are increasing the demand for immigrant labor, both on farms and for caregiving work. In turn, this demographic change creates greater ethnic diversity and increases the potential for intergroup exposure, which results in *both* greater awareness of others and potential conflict.

2.5 Data Framework

The multiple levels depicted in our model of the political communication ecology call for parallel organization in our data analytical framework. For an overview of the data elements presented in the following sections, see Figure 3. There are hundreds of contextual factors at different social levels. Our collection of Wisconsin contextual data spans statewide characteristics and factors at the media market level, such as broadcast political advertising and local news media. We also consider smaller geographic units nested within these larger spaces, such as counties and even zip codes. Our database includes county-level characteristics like employment by industry, mortality and morbidity rates, and specific types of population change. In many cases, our database also contains data at the zip code or census track level. The granularity of this data allows us to: 1) nest individual survey responses at up to six social levels and 2) coordinate these quantitative and computational analyses with the theoretical model

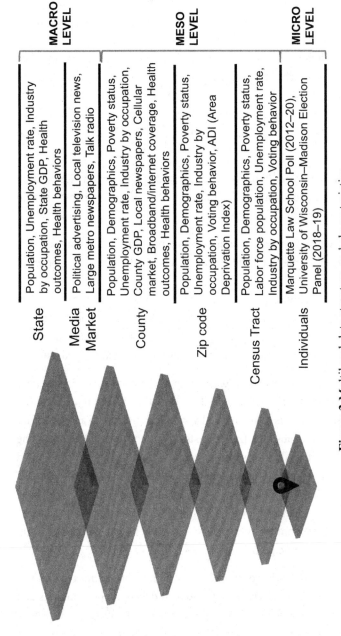

State	Population, Unemployment rate, Industry by occupation, State GDP, Health outcomes, Health behaviors	**MACRO LEVEL**
Media Market	Political advertising, Local television news, Large metro newspapers, Talk radio	
County	Population, Demographics, Poverty status, Unemployment rate, Industry by occupation, County GDP, Local newspapers, Cellular market, Broadband/internet coverage, Health outcomes, Health behaviors	
Zip code	Population, Demographics, Poverty status, Unemployment rate, Industry by occupation, Voting behavior, ADI (Area Deprivation Index)	**MESO LEVEL**
Census Tract	Population, Demographics, Poverty status, Labor force population, Unemployment rate, Industry by occupation, Voting behavior	
Individuals	Marquette Law School Poll (2012–20), University of Wisconsin–Madison Election Panel (2018–19)	**MICRO LEVEL**

Figure 3 Multilevel data structure and characteristics

introduced in this section. This type of attention to context, cross-level inter-actions, and its interplay with shifting media usage and content will be central to the case analyses that follow.

We have operationalized social structure in three stages though first analyzing Wisconsin's changing political–economic, demographic, and sociogeographic landscape and placing it within the historical context of the past forty years (Cramer, 2016; Friedland, 2020). Second, we have used that analysis to select three case studies in which we examine our core theses: that state-level political communication ecology both mediates between national and local-level dis-course and also reflects the uneven terrain of local-level opinions, which emerge out of the intersections of news, state conditions, and local social interactions. The case studies are:

- *Immigration*, a powerfully nationalized issue that powered the Republican ascendency in 2016. It is around this issue that national themes should translate most directly to the state level.

- *Healthcare*, which has also been a point of national contention, but very clearly intersects with both state-level and local, individual-level concerns. Healthcare has been publicly and contentiously debated at the state level in Wisconsin (and many other states), occasioning intense disagreements over Obamacare exchanges, healthcare costs, and Medicaid expansion (which was rejected by Wisconsin's Republican government). But healthcare also most directly impacts the lifeworld decision-making of all individuals and families.

- *A proxy for state economic development*: the debate around the Taiwanese computer manufacturer Foxconn's 2017 proposal to build a manufacturing plant in Wisconsin. This deal, pushed by both Donald Trump and Governor Walker, hinged on subsidies from the state to the tune of $3 billion – the largest tax incentive deal ever proposed for a foreign firm in the United States. Foxconn is a specific case that we use as a proxy for the issue of Walker's state-level economic development ideas and policies. This issue thus connects international-level economic policy to state- and local-level ideas about the economic future of Wisconsin and how it should transform to respond to economic globalization.

Each of these three issues has been a source of contentious politics at the local and state level in Wisconsin, and each stimulated different elite framings and configurations of public and civic contention (Wells et al., 2017).

Third, in our case studies, we draw from the data structure depicted in Figure 3 to model social structure, place, and conversation via a multilevel analysis that explores four major variables –changes in unemployment rates, the changing proportion of the population that is aging, indices of access and quality of healthcare, and the proportion of manufacturing jobs – for all of Wisconsin's seventy-two counties over the one-year period between 2017 and 2018. Building on the approach introduced in Suk et al. (2020), we relate these local contextual conditions to political opinion formation. The evidence is mixed. While we suspect that socioeconomic hardship and sociocultural threat drives people to turn to political extremes, Suk et al. observe the reverse (i.e. that places that show improvement or are more well-off are more polarized and politically extreme). We show how local structures and contexts can create an environment in which some information flows or resources are more available, thus reinforcing certain political attitudes.

2.6 Conclusion

This Element represents a beginning, as we pull together lessons from our ten-year project in order to model a state communication ecology and to frame questions for the future that run throughout each of the sections that follow. We are not generating or testing formal research questions; rather, we are asking a series of broader theoretical and analytical questions, and using our data to create descriptive models that can illuminate the following problems.

First, we try to understand the dynamics and degree of nationalization. Does it flow from the top, or do the civic fractures that give rise to hyperpolarized political and social life operate differently at multiple levels? In the case sections that follow – on immigration, healthcare, and economic development – we show that even while being driven by a national media system, issues take different shapes according to social geography and lived experience.

Second, we want to understand how the state and local levels of the hybrid media system change the flow of discourse and opinion. Some issues appear to be more 'nationalized' than others. We will also demonstrate how the degree of an issue's nationalization is reflected in mediated discourse about that issue.

Third, as Benkler et al. (2018) have demonstrated, the hybrid media system is split into two large clusters, a partisan right-wing and a mainstream that includes both center and left news. We ask how this structural difference is manifest at the state level. In particular, in each case section we illustrate the pattern of connections among different parts of the media system for a given issue domain.

Fourth, for each case we ask what conventional discourses Wisconsinites use to talk about immigration, healthcare, and the economy. How do they vary? Where possible, we also show the connections between framing devices and conventional discourses.

Fifth, we connect how individual personal characteristics, exposure to political information, and local contexts combine to shape individuals' opinions on political issues.

Finally, we ask: How does the embeddedness of issues in the everyday lifeworld of social actors shape or modify opinion? Does embeddedness modify partisanship?

These interlocking issues – economic decline, rural vs. urban identities, healthcare, and immigration – run through this Element. However, as each of the substantive sections show, none of these issues are as simple as "national political parties set agendas and priorities, which are communicated downward through national communication systems." Section 3 explains our data domain, strategy of analysis, and methods. Section 4, "Immigration," illustrates the limits of nationalizing discourse. Section 5, "Healthcare," shows how political frames are shaped from above and what happens when these frames come up against citizens' contradictory lifeworld experiences. Section 6, "Foxconn and Economic Development," demonstrates how variations in social position, partisanship, and geography intersect to create more complexity in political opinion than standard accounts allow.

3 Studying the Wisconsin Communication Ecology

with Josephine Lukito (*University of Texas–Austin*), Sadie Dempsey (*University of Wisconsin–Madison*), Jiyoun Suk (*University of Connecticut*), Jianing Li (*University of Wisconsin–Madison*), Ellie Yang (*University of Wisconsin–Madison*), Jordan M. Foley (Washington State University), Ceri Hughes (Cardiff University), Monica Sansonetti Busch (*University of Wisconsin–Madison*), Zhongkai Sun (Amazon), Zening Duan (*University of Wisconsin–Madison*), and Charles Franklin (Marquette University)

As a research team, we have been studying Wisconsin's political communication ecology for ten years, gathering, assembling, cleaning, and integrating data from a variety of sources – work that informs this Element's approach to the questions developed in Section 2. Using survey and conversational data, our previous work has described how Wisconsin's contentious politics prefigured the populist presidential election of 2016. For example, we found that Wisconsin media provided Republicans with solidarity signals to link their vote choice for governor to traits of decisiveness and authority – traits that Democrats were less likely to value (Wagner et al., 2014). Cramer's (2016) analysis of conversational data highlighted the role that geography, resentment, and social identity played in the contemporary political divisions defining Wisconsin – and, by extension, many other parts of the United States. We also found that after the 2011–12 debates over Act 10, which abolished public worker bargaining, more than one-third of Wisconsinites cut off conversations with those in their social, professional, and political networks whose views differed on the recall election of former Governor Scott Walker (Wells et al., 2017). More recently, we combined layers of these data to shed light on various complex problems: Trump supporters' news use (Dempsey et al., 2020), whether improving economic and social conditions at the contextual level hardens partisan preferences (Suk et al., 2020), and how media use, talk networks, and anti-elitism vary across Wisconsin's social and regional geography (Wells et al., 2021).

In the past decade, we also have made contributions in the area of methodological innovations, using computational tools, natural language processing, time-series modeling, and other techniques for estimating temporal dynamics and communication influence (Shah et al., 2002, Shah et al., 2005; Shah et al., 2015; Wells et al., 2016, 2019). Combined with qualitative analyses of in-depth interviews and ethnographic fieldwork to understand and connect the various layers of Wisconsin's communication ecology (Cramer, 2016; Dempsey et al., 2020), our approach allows us to examine how those layers affect and respond to a variety of political and civic outcomes.

In this Element, we undertake a more comprehensive and integrative set of analyses than we have yet presented for the Wisconsin case. In each of the three following sections, the reader will encounter a multi-method analysis of the behavior of Wisconsin's communication ecology around a specific issue – immigration (Section 4), healthcare (Section 5), and the economy (Section 6). For consistency of analysis and clarity of presentation, the data collected and methods used are parallel across the sections, and are presented in the same order in each case. This section serves as an overarching description of our data collection processes and methods, which were replicated for each issue.

Let us begin with an overview of the datasets we constructed for this project. Building on the notion of a statewide communication ecology (laid out in Section 2), we aimed to capture communications occurring at multiple locations within that ecology, from the personal opinions and interpersonal communications that occurred in informal political talk, to the contents of formal news media such as newspapers, to the messages and ideas circulating in social media and promoted by political/media elites, actors, and average citizens. This led us to assemble several sets of data, which we analyze and synthesize throughout this Element (See Figure 4):

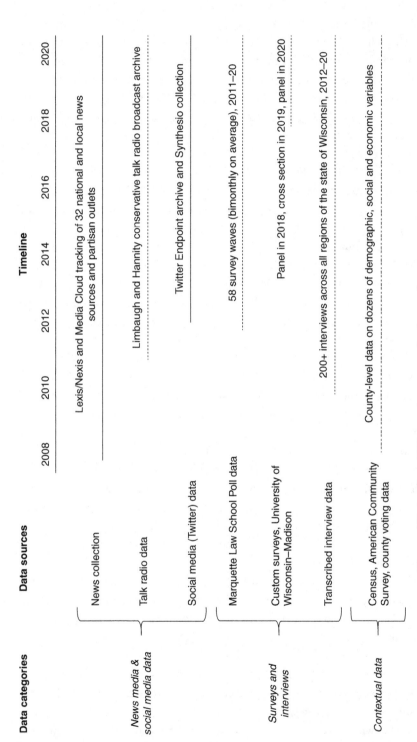

Figure 4 Data map of Wisconsin communication ecology components

- Semi-structured interviews with 228 residents across the state.
- Two dozen interviews with Wisconsin media and political elites from both parties.
- Content from national and local news media across thirty-four media outlets, ranging from local newspapers to national partisan media, including conservative talk radio.
- An archive of sixty billion Twitter messages from 2012 to the present, tens of millions of which pertain to Wisconsin politics and political elites.
- Fifty-eight waves of the Marquette University Law School poll of statewide opinion from 2011 and custom panel surveys of Wisconsin residents around the 2018 and 2020 elections.
- Country-level contextual data on dozens of demographic, social, and economic factors.

Put briefly, our analytic approach was to begin with the inductive, rich, and descriptive evidence provided by our qualitative interview methods, then examine these relationships more formally with the representative data offered by our news and social media content and survey data. The 228 interviews with Wisconsin residents yielded a wealth of data about how citizens in the state talk about the issues of immigration, healthcare, and the economy; to analyze the ideas and the recurrent, vernacular, ready-made points about political issues that our respondents used in conversation, we use Strauss' (2012) notion of "conventional discourses."

To move between everyday citizen discourse and other forms of media, we used the conventional discourse markers collected from these conversations and searched for versions and variations of them circulating on Twitter in conversations about Wisconsin politics surrounding key national elites and local actors (i.e. emanating from them, mentioning them, or directed at them). We also searched for these conventional discourses across the thirty-four local and national news sources and partisan media outlets, examining the presence of frame devices that reflect these discourses. In both cases, we coded for the basic ideas embedded in conventional discourses using syntax tagging, dictionary approaches, and supervised machine learning, as described in Section 3.1. Figure 5 displays this process.

We track these comparable ways of talking about issues in order to operationalize discursive power and measure its presence across the communication ecology (see Section 2 and Jungherr et al., 2019): Using these tactics, we examine how citizens, operating through and amplifying elite voices using social media, interact with news media discourses. The approach we advance allows us to analyze how citizens' social media discourses both reflect and

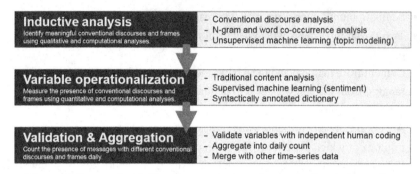

Figure 5 Conventional discourse analysis and computational text coding

shape news media, and how they might ultimately sway public opinion on topics like immigration, healthcare, and the economy. Using time-series analysis to examine temporal dynamics, we examine patterns of discursive commonality and flow among national legacy and partisan media, local and regional Wisconsin newspapers, conservative talk radio, national and local Wisconsin elites on Twitter, and broader social media discourses and search patterns. Examining the flows of discourse provides insight into how conventional discourses and frame devices move within and among communication platforms: vertically, from the national to the local level; asymmetrically, from partisan sources; and selectively, by issue ownership and local resonance.

Finally, we expect that these discourses' power will come from their dissemination through media coupled with patterns of audience consumption of these outlets. That is, individual patterns of legacy and local news use, partisan media diet, social media network characteristics, and conversational ties – depending on the prevalence of certain discourses in these sources as well as factors related to citizens' local contexts – will sway opinion on issues such as immigration, healthcare, and economic development. This interplay of the temporal and contextual also reflects a broader theme of our analytic approach.

To summarize: the reader will find in each of the following three sections a progression of three analyses. First, we present the results of conventional discourse analysis in the form of a distilled description of the discourses citizens used in interviews. Second, we display time-series models investigating over-time relationships in the prominence of key conventional discourses among specific actors in social media and news media. Third, via multilevel modeling of survey responses, we show how citizens' opinions about our three key issues are related to their exposure to media and the framing devices they contain, as well as their social-structural positions and local contexts.

We now turn to the methodological details of these analyses.

3.1 Inductive Analysis

We identified conventional discourses and frame devices through analysis of three data sources.

Interview data. We began with qualitative conventional discourse analysis of interviews. We conducted in-person, semi-structured interviews with 228 people living in Wisconsin. We purposively sought interviews with a diverse range of participants, with respect to gender (women: 112; men: 116), race and ethnicity (white: 163; nonwhite: 65, including Oneida, Menominee, Black, Middle Eastern, Latinx, and Asian-American), geographic location (all 8 congressional districts, with 60 percent of those interviewed from rural areas or outstate cities), and political ideology (Democrats or liberals: 91; Republicans or conservatives: 54; Independent or moderate: 83). Whenever possible, interviews were conducted in naturally occurring groups grounded in community associations or occupations, allowing us to observe group dynamics and interactions and providing richer interview data for our analysis. It is in these data that our search for conventional discourses in social media and associated frame devices in news content began.

News media data. We began constructing our local news corpus by collecting all stories about Wisconsin politics published between 2016 and 2018 in seven outlets: *The Sheboygan Press, Milwaukee Journal Sentinel, Green Bay Press Gazette, Fond Du Lac Reporter, The Northwestern, Stevens Point Journal,* and *Wisconsin Rapids Daily Tribune.*

We also tracked national legacy news media sources and partisan outlets using Media Cloud (Benkler et al., 2018). These included nine liberal outlets (*Daily Beast, Daily Kos, Huffington, MSNBC, Newsweek, NPR, Raw Story, Slate,* and *Vox*), nine moderate sources, which included legacy news media (*ABC, CNN, The Hill, New York Times, Politico, RealClearPolitics, USA Today, Washington Post,* and *Wall Street Journal*), and seven conservative outlets (*Breitbart, Daily Caller, Fox News, Gateway, InfoWars, Washington Times,* and *Washington Examiner*). Using Media Cloud, we also tracked Rush Limbaugh's and Sean Hannity's conservative talk radio programs, bringing the total of conservative sources to nine.

Social media data. For social media, we focused on Twitter activity from 2016 to 2018. Starting in July 2016, we used the social listening service Synthesio, which collects data from a Twitter decahose stream. Our search string of Wisconsin keywords yielded 10,233,094 posts via Synthesio (see Appendix 1: Synthesio Search Terms – all appendices are available at https://mcrc .journalism.wisc.edu/battleground-appendices/).

We next divided the interview, news media, and social media corpora based on the three topics of interest using case-insensitive substring searches. For immigration, we used the following keywords: immigra* (to capture "immigration" and "immigrant" and other related words), dreamer, illegals, undocumented, and alien. For healthcare, we used: healthcare, health care, affordable care act, aca, Obamacare, health coverage, medical coverage, medicare, and medicaid. For economic development, we began with the term "walker" to focus on the Governor's efforts to create jobs, a key campaign commitment, which was then combined with other economic development terms, before narrowing to focus on his signature policy goal, securing Foxconn with massive tax incentives. This produced nine corpora: one interview corpus, one news media corpus, and one social media corpus for each topic.

Conventional discourses. A conventional discourse has two components: a shared schema, or simplified understanding of the world, and rhetoric that is easy to grasp and repeat (Strauss, 2012). Conventional discourses are acquired through opinion communities, including social networks and the media. Our aim in identifying and tracing conventional discourses is to better understand how people express political viewpoints in everyday life – expressions that, as Strauss (2012) has shown, can be quite varied and even mutually contradictory. We qualitatively identified conventional discourses in our own interview data related to immigration, healthcare, and economic development. We created an index with a comprehensive list of each conventional discourse, along with their underlying schemas, the rhetoric used, and examples of each. We then selected conventional discourses from this index for inclusion in the case studies using two criteria. First, we chose conventional discourses that were most prevalent across our data layers. Second, we aimed to include conventional discourses that exist on a particular side of the partisan divide as well as those that are present across the ideological spectrum. We deemed our analysis complete when the conventional discourse index for a topic was saturated (i.e. when we could not identify new conventional discourses to add). We then applied the same inductive qualitative approach to a random sample of 1,000 tweets and 100 news stories containing the topic keywords. The index of terms was expanded with examples from these text data. In this way, we aimed to systematically identify conventional discourse and corresponding frame devices in these different data layers while attending to the way they change across them.

The qualitative analysis of Twitter and news media was further supplemented with several computer-assisted analyses, including n-gram analyses, semantic network maps, and structural topic modeling. These were used to identify conventional discourses that were not already included in our index and to isolate pervasive language patterns that occurred for specific conventional discourses. For the news data, we were interested in how conventional discourses were presented as message frames in newspaper articles. We examined three layers of frames: cue frames in words or phrases, statement frames in sentences, and argument frames in paragraphs and quotes (McLeod and Shah, 2015). In total, we identified three conventional discourses/frame devices for immigration, three for healthcare, and five for Walker and economic development plans tied to Foxconn. These discourses are discussed in detail in each of the sections that follow.

3.2 Variable Operationalization

We used our indices of conventional discourses to operationalize quantitative measures in two ways. First, we constructed several annotated dictionaries of linguistic markers representing conventional discourses in social media and news frames in journalistic content by identifying syntactical and lexical patterns that were common among the examples of conventional discourses in our index. Syntax patterns, such as the use of a modal with a specific subject or object (e.g. "the United States must"), were essential to include because syntax annotations improve the computer's understanding of language structure (Shah et al., 2002). This also allowed us to exclude negations (e.g. "Obamacare is not good for America"). We then used these dictionaries to code our six corpora of social media messages and news articles for the presence or absence of conventional discourses and frame devices.

Our second approach used a supervised machine learning strategy to label social media messages for negative sentiment. We constructed a training set with three undergraduate students manually coding for negative sentiment in 15,000 social media messages (11,808 were tweets). To build the classifier, we selected the base-uncased-BERT (Bidirectional Encoder Representation from Transformers), an advanced language model pre-trained on large-scale corpora and publicly available in Python, and employed 5-fold cross-validation to avoid over-fitting (89 percent accuracy and an F1-score of 0.88). Both the dictionary method and the supervised machine learning strategy labeled the corpora at the message level.

Wisconsin elite accounts: We further subdivided the coded Twitter content into posts surrounding elite Wisconsin accounts (i.e. created by, mentioning, or directed to them), separating these out from the broader Twitter discourses. To identify elite accounts, we used multiple rounds of snowball sampling, seeded with known political accounts, to generate a list of over 1,000 highly visible Wisconsin political and media elite accounts for two years, 2012 and 2020. The authors reviewed the lists and retained all accounts that appeared in both sets and had a follower count over 500. Consequential accounts that did not appear on both lists were retained or added if they maintained a large follower count and remained active through the study period of 2016 to 2018; 775 of these accounts were included. The authors then coded these accounts for whether they represented a national or local political elite, whether it reflected a conservative, moderate/nonpartisan, or liberal ideology, and what type of individual or institution ran the account (for details of the coding of individual accounts and the overall composition of coded elite accounts, including follower and following counts, see Appendix 2: Elite Wisconsin Twitter Accounts, https://mcrc.journalism.wisc.edu/battleground-appendices/).

To verify that our national accounts were higher in status and potential influence than our local accounts, we compared the follower and following counts of conservative, moderate/nonpartisan, and liberal accounts at different levels. The national accounts, which included Governor Walker, US Senators Baldwin and Johnson, and Paul Ryan (then Speaker of the House of Representatives) had a much higher mean follower count than the local accounts (421,088 vs. 7,485, respectively). However, there was considerable asymmetry in this pattern. The eight national Wisconsin political elite accounts we identified on the right averaged 556,506 followers, and the two liberal accounts averaged 28,493 followers. This was not the case at the local level, where the 162 accounts identified as conservative averaged 6,607 followers and the 232 accounts identified as liberal averaged 8,735 followers. The ratio of followers to following is similarly asymmetrical at the national elite level, with conservatives, on average, having higher follower-to-following ratios. For clarity, these Twitter elites at the local level are referred to as *political actors* to differentiate them from national elites centered in Wisconsin such as US Senators Baldwin and Johnson.

3.3 Times-Series Analysis

Time-series aggregation. Once we had the data coded at the message level, we aggregated the data temporally, counting the number of news articles or social media messages that contained a given conventional discourse by day. We used the timestamp metadata embedded in the news corpora and social media corpora (see Appendix 3: Discourse Counts by Media, https://mcrc .journalism.wisc.edu/battleground-appendices/).

We further subdivided the coded Twitter content into content by and about our elite sources, as distinguished from other discourse. We grouped the content under the broad categories of national conservative elites, national liberal elites, local conservative actors, local moderate/nonpartisan actors, and local liberal actors. Notably, there were no Wisconsin national political elites who were moderate or nonpartisan, so this category was omitted. The partisan categories were mainly made up of politicians, political appointees, and advocacy groups, while most of the moderate/nonpartisan sources were media entities, government agencies, and local journalists. To capture all content surrounding these accounts, in addition to the posts emanating from them, we also aggregated posts that retweeted content from the accounts, replied to them, or otherwise engaged with them through quoting or @mentioning. All content under these categories was combined when aggregating discourse layers.

Event timelines. We constructed event timelines for each topic using a combination of deductive and inductive processes. First, we inductively identified significant political, legislative, and economic events occurring during the period and clustered them into various categories. We derived these categories based on activity at the federal and state level that substantially changed the status quo within the topic area. With a few exceptions, these events were identified based on primary sources of government activity (such as the submission of legislation, a change in policy, or a judicial decision). Sources based on media coverage were used only in combination with official sources and were primarily used to cross-validate timelines from other organizations (e.g. American Civil Liberties Union [ACLU], American Immigration Lawyers Association [AILA], etc.). These procedures ensured that our initial batch of events were exogenous to our data on news and social media discourse.

We supplemented the event timelines with additional events identified using a time-series outlier analyses of the news data, which identified significant peaks in the volume of news coverage on each topic. This enabled us to identify specific time points when a topic reached high salience in the news agenda, indicating events that might otherwise have been missed in the inductive process. Only a few events were discovered using the outlier analyses, and were only included if we found a single, clearly identifiable event (on the day before or after the peak) that would otherwise have met the criteria for inclusion during our inductive process. If multiple potential events occurred within that time window, or if we could identify none at all, we did not add the event to the dataset. (For details of the coding of the event timelines, see Appendix 4: Issue Timelines for Immigration, Health Care, and Economic Development, https://mcrc.journalism.wisc.edu/battleground-appendices/).

Time-series modeling: We conducted a series of time-series regressions using the Prais-Winsten approach to account for autocorrelation (Prais and Winsten, 1954). Our time series for these models are pre-whitened, meaning that fractionally integrated data-generating components are removed (this is a common procedure for time series; see Vogelsang, 1998). For each topic, we calculated 30 to 43 models for the following daily variables:

(a) every frame device in national conservative, moderate, and liberal news outlets and in national conservative talk radio;
(b) the corresponding conventional discourses on Twitter surrounding national Wisconsin conservative elites and Wisconsin national liberal elites;
(c) parallel conventional discourses surrounding local conservative actors, local moderate actors, and local liberal actors;
(d) the parallel frame devices in local news media;
(e) conventional discourses in all other Twitter content in each corpus; and
(f) Google search volume for related terms.

The goal of these time-series models was to examine patterns of communication co-occurrence within this hybrid system, not to tease out causal relationships or assert specific triggers of influence. Rather, our goal is to understand discursive power, asymmetry, and the interplay between national and state forces when operating across the three issues of immigration, healthcare, and state economic development centered on Foxconn.

For each model, we included the following as independent variables: (a) timeline variables specific to that issue domain (e.g. release of monthly state unemployment data for the economic development timeline) to account for factors driving all discourses, and (b) frame devices in national conservative, moderate, and liberal news outlets, as well as conservative talk radio, omitting the media frame category being predicted. From here, additional fully saturated models were tested, with the presence of each frame device or conventional discourse taking its turn as the dependent variable; we sequentially introduced into the model the frames and discourses surrounding Twitter elites and local actors, in local newspaper content, across general Wisconsin Twitter discourse, and as reflected in the volume of Google search terms. The inclusion of media variables as both *dependent variables* (in their own model for other frame devices or conventional discourses) and *independent variables* (in models where corresponding variables were the dependent variable) allowed us to identify bidirectional relationships. This approach aligns with preexisting literature on social and news media interrelationships without preassuming untested relationships. In addition to the modeling of several media layers, it is notable that we disaggregate activity within these media layers into different discourses. The full output of all 105 models can be found in Appendix 5: Time-Series Logs for Immigration (Table 1_1 to Table 1_32), Healthcare (Table 2_1 to Table 2_30), and Economic Development/Foxconn Analysis (Table 3_1 to Table 3_43), https://mcrc.journalism.wisc.edu/battleground-appendices/.

Following this modeling, we combined the results of our models using a nondirected network illustration of relationships, using the media layers as the nodes and the simultaneous use of discourses (i.e. the results of the time-series regressions) as the edges. Due to the overwhelming number of relationships identified within these models, we focus our analysis on the following relationships: those that are very unlikely to be true under a null hypothesis ($p < 0.01$) and those that occur repeatedly across multiple discourses (i.e. have more than one statistically significant relationship; Vargo and Guo, 2017). From this, we constructed two visualizations, one focusing on the partisan flows of this discourse, and one aggregating the partisanship of each media layer; together, these visualizations depict a distilled form of the media ecology. We see these visualizations as *snapshots of communication flows and discursive power* for each of the issues circulating in the state communication ecology during the time of our analysis. The full set of these figures (included in Appendix 6: Time-Series Visualizations, https://mcrc .journalism.wisc.edu/battleground-appendices/) offers a summary of the key relationships among elements of the communication ecology in the following sections.

3.4 Multilevel Modeling and Media Content Integration

To understand how local context features, media flows, and communication patterns are related to Wisconsinites' perceptions of issues and policies, we used a web-based survey panel collected in October 2018 and December 2018, focusing on registered voters in Wisconsin. The survey sample was stratified according to geographic regions and demographics to represent the Wisconsin population, resulting in a total number of 2,058 respondents in wave one (which we focus on in this Element). The media content information from the time-series analysis was the basis for estimating flows of communication to individual respondents, by creating an algorithm that considered the sources of respondents' media diet combined with the amount of coded discourse carried by that source, which we detail below. In the dataset, individuals are nested within seventy-two counties in Wisconsin; therefore, we integrated our analysis using multilevel modeling for two reasons: to account for both individual-level and county-level variances, and to consider how media diet, content flows, and social context intersect.

County-level variables: For county-level features, we looked at four variables of contextual changes: shifts in unemployment rates; proportion of older population; index of access and quality of healthcare; and proportion of manufacturing jobs from 2017 to 2018 (see Figure 6).

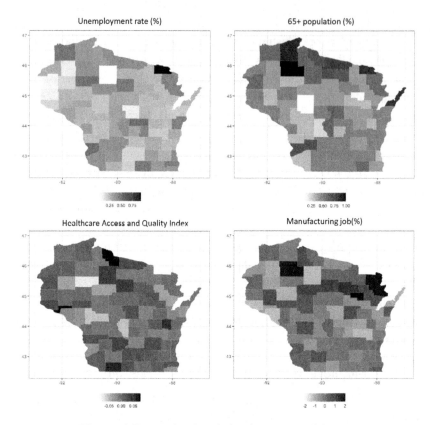

Figure 6 County-level variation in contextual factors

Unemployment rate percentage data for each county were obtained from the Bureau of Labor Statistics of the US Department of Labor.[3] The proportion of manufacturing jobs data was gathered from the American Community Survey conducted by the US Census Bureau, as was information about population graying: the percentage of older (65+) Wisconsinites in each county.[4] Finally, we obtained data calculating an index (1 to 100) for each county's access to and quality of

---

[3] The change in unemployment rates between 2017 and 2018 was created by subtracting the 2018 rate from the 2017 rate, so that higher values indicate the improvement in unemployment over the one-year period. Note that the improvement in unemployment rate does not necessarily correspond to the urbanization of counties; for example, Florence County, one of the rural counties in Wisconsin, witnessed the sharpest decrease in unemployment – from 4.7 percent in 2017 to 3.8 percent in 2018. In Dane County, a metro core county that is home to the state capital, the change in unemployment rate over the one-year period was minimal (absolute rate change of 0.15 percent, with the unemployment rate remaining under 2.5 percent). Milwaukee County, another metro core in Wisconsin, ranks twelfth (out of seventy-two) in improvement in unemployment (4.02 percent in 2017 and 3.63 percent in 2018).

[4] The variables were constructed by calculating an absolute percent change between 2017 and 2018 estimates. Overall, rural counties show higher proportions of the 65+ population (about 20 percent on

healthcare from health-ranking reports of the University of Wisconsin–Madison's Population Health Institute.[5] These four factors varied considerably across the state and were not highly interrelated, suggesting potentially discrete contextual influences that may shape attitudes about immigration, healthcare, and the economy.

Individual-level variables*: Estimated media exposure to immigration, healthcare, and Foxconn discourses.* We used the following procedures to compute an index of exposure to discourses about each set of issues through various types of media sources over the one-month period prior to the survey. We employed identical processes across all issues; here, the immigration issue is used as a procedural example.

First, we took account of the decay of media effects over time by applying decay rates to the observed daily frequency of each immigration discourse in each of the media sources over the one-month period. Following De Vreese et al. (2017) and Wojcieszak and Garrett (2018), and informed by the time-series analysis, we assumed that news media and talk radio content decays at a 0.8 rate per day and social media content decays at a 0.5 rate per day. Next, for each source on a given day, we calculated the prevalence of specific discourses relative to competing discourses by subtracting the latter from the former (both adjusted for decay rates); the daily scores were then summed over the one-month period for each source.

In the survey, we asked respondents how often in the last week they had used media content from a range of twenty-seven sources (1 = never, 5 = very often;

---

average; Vilas County has the highest percentage of the 65+ population, at 29.4 percent in 2017 and 30.2 percent in 2018) than urban counties. Our data further shows that many of the rural counties in northern Wisconsin experienced the highest growth in the 65+ population. Notably, many counties in Wisconsin, including both rural areas and some urban clusters, rely heavily on manufacturing jobs; for example, more than 30 percent of jobs (in both 2017 and 2018) in Sheboygan, Price, and Manitowoc counties are manufacturing jobs. However, counties show variances in changes in manufacturing jobs. While Dane and Milwaukee, the two metro cores in Wisconsin, show relatively stable employment in manufacturing jobs, rural counties and some urban clusters show variation in changes in manufacturing jobs, ranging from an increase by 2 (raw percentage change) in Menominee County to a decrease by 2 (raw percentage change) in Florence County.

[5] The reports provided standardized scores of healthcare access and quality measures, based on the equal weighting of access to care (the percentage of uninsured population, ratio of population to primary care physicians, and ratio of population to dentists) and quality of care (number of preventable hospital stays, percentage of diabetic Medicare enrollees that receive HbA1c blood sugar monitoring, and percentage of female Medicare enrollees by age that receive mammography screening). The suburban ring areas (counties contiguous to Milwaukee – Waukesha, Ozaukee, and Washington counties) as well as Dane County, generally show greater access to and quality of healthcare services than the average of all counties, according to the standardized index. These counties ranked high in both 2017 and 2018, with their index measures remaining largely unchanged across the one-year period, whereas some rural counties like Florence showed a drop in the healthcare access and quality index, going from above the average to below the average in that year.

M = 1.82, SD = 0.55). We multiplied the self-reported media use frequency (rescaled to 0–1) with the measure of the prevalence of this discourse for each corresponding source. For example, for the immigration issue, the estimated score for *CNN* is the product of the self-reported use of *CNN* and the prevalence of the "national security" immigration discourse and the "legalization" immigration discourse (both of which were critical of relaxing immigration standards) relative to the "humanitarian" discourse (which argued for fair treatment of immigrants) in *CNN* over the one-month period.

Finally, media sources were clustered together to create the index. The index of liberal media was created by averaging *MSNBC, NPR, Daily Beast, Newsweek, Slate, Huffington Post, Vox, Raw Story,* and *Daily Kos.* The index of moderate media was created by averaging *ABC, New York Times, Washington Post, CNN, Politico, USA Today, The Hill, Wall Street Journal,* and *RealClearPolitics.* The index of conservative media was created by averaging *Fox News, Washington Examiner, Daily Caller, InfoWars, Breitbart, Gateway Pundit,* and *Washington Times.* The index of local newspapers was created by averaging The *Sheboygan Press, Milwaukee Journal Sentinel, Green Bay Press Gazette, Fond Du Lac Reporter, The Northwestern, Stevens Point Journal,* and *Wisconsin Rapids Daily Tribune.* Twitter was a stand-alone measure. The index of conservative talk radio was created by averaging Sean Hannity and Rush Limbaugh.

Having at least one Republican talk partner. We asked respondents to identify three people with whom they had discussed matters important to them over the last six months. We asked how respondents perceived the partisanship of each talk partner. We created a dummy variable for whether a respondent had at least one talk partner who was perceived as leaning toward the Republican Party, a Republican, or a strong Republican (1 = yes [46.18 percent], 0 = no [53.82 percent]).

Partisanship. We asked respondents to report their partisan identification (for respondents identified as Independents or Other, they were asked whether they leaned more toward the Republican Party, the Democratic Party, or neither). We recoded the items to a 7-point scale (1 = Strong Democrat, 7 = Strong Republican; M = 4.07, SD = 2.02).

Demographic information. Respondents reported their age (M = 55.2, SD = 14.9); gender (49.1% female), education level (18.0% high school or less, 20.1% some college, 13.4% associate degree, 31.5% bachelor's degree, 17.0% advanced degree); household income (46.8% in the range $25,000 to $74,999); and race/ethnicity (92.1% white).

Measures of policy opinions: These variables were structured to predict opinion about immigration, healthcare, and economic development, beginning with models that tested the relationship of demographic and communication variables with the outcome measures. Next, the four contextual-level factors were added to each set of hierarchical linear models (HLM). Finally, cross-level interactions were estimated; these estimates took account of how local context may moderate the relationship between exposure to issue discourse in news media or social media and citizens' issue attitudes. Throughout the analysis, we grand-mean centered the county-level variables and group-mean centered the individual-level variables, following Enders and Tofighi (2007). The full set of model runs, as well as additional details on the estimation of the media exposure via content integration, are included in Appendix 7: HLM Construction and Comparisons, https://mcrc.journalism.wisc.edu/battleground-appendices/.

3.5 Methodological Synthesis and Appendices

All time-series modeling and multilevel modeling is presented in the appendices to this section (available at https://mcrc.journalism.wisc.edu/battleground-appendices/). Readers may wish to examine these specific relationships in detail. However, our focus in the coming sections of this Element is not on reviewing all the information contained in the rich archive of interview data we have collected, nor on examining the relationships between specific discourses that move across the media ecology. Rather, in keeping with our theoretical interest in questions concerning the communication ecology itself, the sections focus on broader patterns and conclusions drawn from these analyses.

Consistent with this approach, the relationships among aspects of the national and local communication ecology are summarized in the figures presented in the subsequent sections. The relationships between aspects of the communication ecology in terms of discourse flows concerning immigration are illustrated in Figure 7 (Section 4) (which condenses thirty-two Prais-Winsten regressions in Appendix 5, Table 1_1 to Table 1_32). Figure 10 (Section 5) does the same for healthcare discourse flows based on thirty Prais-Winsten regressions (Appendix 5, Table 2_1 to Table 2_30). Foxconn discourse relationships are depicted in Figure 13 (Section 5) (this summarizes forty-three Prais-Winsten regressions in Appendix 5, Table 3_1 to Table 3_43). Many event and discourse-specific relationships merit unpacking, but the theoretical scope of this Element forces a more summative approach.

The same is true for the multilevel modeling, from which key relationships, including cross-level interactions, are highlighted in figures and tables (the larger tables contain the output of the full multiple HLM models presented in Appendix 7). Specifically, the models concerning public opinion about immigration, of which key findings are depicted in Figures 8 and 9 (Section 4), can be found in Appendix 7, Table 1_A to Table 1_C. Figures 11 and 12 (Section 5) do the same for public opinion concerning healthcare, highlighting key relationships from the regressions in Appendix 7, Table 2_A to Table 2_C. Key relationships concerning public opinion about Wisconsin's economic prospects are illustrated in Figure 14 (Section 6), with the full HLM regressions in Appendix 7, Table 3_A and Table 3_B.

In each section, we first offer our sense, informed by insights from hundreds of interviews and dozens of time-series model specifications, of how citizens make sense of these issues and the ways in which discursive power operates within the communication system. We then present the results of testing multi-level models that consider changes in local context alongside media and communication flows. Then, by looking across these three issues, we are able to generate inferences about the communication ecology.

4 Immigration: Complex Issues and Conservative Asymmetries

with Jiyoun Suk (*University of Connecticut*), Josephine Lukito (*University of Texas–Austin*), Sadie Dempsey (*University of Wisconsin–Madison*), and Jianing Li (*University of Wisconsin–Madison*)

Anna and Leo are strong Republicans living in Wisconsin's WOW counties (Washington, Ozaukee, and Waukesha), the state's conservative stronghold just outside the city of Milwaukee. Anna, a woman in her late fifties, became a Republican activist to support Wisconsin Governor Scott Walker during the recall election in 2011. Her wavy blonde hair frames her face, falling just above the neck of her "When is it my turn to get offended?" T-shirt. Leo is an avid Trump supporter, wearing a dark blue "American Dreamer" MAGA ("Make America Great Again") hat – one of many in his expanding collection. When the conversation turned to immigration, Anna began with a familiar conservative refrain:

Anna: I think you're not a country if you can't control your borders. Why are we letting in these bad people? If you're a good person and you have something to contribute, like intelligence, maybe you can write, you have something you could give to the promotion of this country that we built. And why are we letting people that are already admitting that they're going to destroy it.

Leo: Bring them in here then you give them free stuff like Obamacare.

Anna: I know it. Oh my gosh! And don't get me started on all that free stuff because there's a lot of it. I mean, I don't even … These Obama phones. I mean, everything is better than what we're using and we're

the ones paying for it. But back to the point. You know the immigrants
and the country . . . Ellis Island. We're all immigrants or descendants
of immigrants, right? I mean, seriously . . . They had rules. If you had
disease or you had something that was going to potentially harm the
people here, they didn't let you in, at least for a while. And that was
okay, right?

At first glance, this may sound like typical logic from devoted Republican
partisans. Anna's initial remarks criticize the United States for "letting in these
bad people" whose aim is to "destroy" the country. She and Leo then lament
immigrants getting "free stuff" (i.e. government assistance). However, Anna's
anti-immigrant sentiment is attenuated later in the conversation as she adds
nuance to her argument. For example, she distinguishes good people from bad
people, emphasizing that the former includes immigrants who have historically
come to the United States through Ellis Island. This evocation describes the
United States as a nation of immigrants, normalizing the inclusion of immigrants
as part of US history. For a moment, we see Anna oscillating between anti-
immigrant sentiments and more moderate sentiments about the conditions under
which immigration is acceptable to her, specifying that those who want to
contribute to American society through their intelligence or other capabilities
should be allowed to immigrate. Anna is here intertwining anti-immigrant conventional discourses with pro-immigrant ones. We see this interweaving of pro-
and anti-immigrant discourses across our interviews, but it tends to be particularly
prevalent in our interviews with conservatives like Anna and Leo.

Immigration has become a hyper-partisan issue over the past decade in the
United States, reaching a peak during and after the 2016 Presidential election
(Gimpel, 2019). The then-candidate Donald Trump made immigration a key
plank of his platform with his mantra of "build the wall" – a phrase that
encapsulated his attitudes to immigration policy. His anti-immigration sentiment was front and center in his Wisconsin rallies, where Trump described
Madison and Milwaukee as "sanctuary cities" providing safe havens to
'illegal immigrants." However, Wisconsin residents' attitudes toward immigration are complicated by the state's dairy industry, which relies heavily on
immigrant labor (Perez, 2019). In this section, we explore the role of the
communication ecology in shaping attitudes about immigration policy. Our
analysis highlights an asymmetry between immigration rhetoric and discourse frames in partisan media and those used by citizens in their own local
conversations; this shows that while national news does influence public
opinion about immigration, local context moderates that influence.

4.1 Immigration Conventional Discourses

While there are a range of conventional discourses related to immigration, we focus here on three of the most prominent and reoccurring ones. Following the approach proposed by Strauss (2012), we analyze the following: (1) *national security,* (2) *immigration requires rules,* and (3) *humanitarian* conventional discourses. These discourses represent a broad spectrum of opinion about (and discussions of) immigration, and were the most frequently occurring discourses in our data set. We analyze these three discourses through an exploratory, mixed-methods analysis of interview data, social media content, and news articles.

We observed the *national security* discourse in statements expressing anti-immigrant sentiment. The underlying schema of this discourse is the belief that immigrants, particularly illegal immigrants, are a potential threat to the safety and security of American citizens and that citizens can only be protected from this threat through strict immigration policy and strong borders.

Anna drew on this conventional discourse when she said, "I think you're not a country if you can't control your borders. Why are we letting in these bad people?" This quote highlights two related beliefs: first, that some immigrants are "bad people" who are a danger to the nation and, second, that not "control-[ling] your borders" poses a threat to the country. This is an important conditional statement that makes border protection a precondition for a country's existence. The target of Anna's frustration is twofold: her anger is targeted first at the "bad people" who are immigrating illegally and second at the government ("we") for allowing these "bad people" to breach the country's borders. Anna mentioned "potential harm" as a key reason why (certain) immigrants should not be allowed into the United States. This notion of harm was also repeated by others employing this conventional discourse; they highlighted violence (particularly rape and murder), drug dealing, and diseases as reasons to oppose immigration.

While the *national security* conventional discourse is generally used to express anti-immigration sentiment, *immigration requires rules* can be used to express either pro- or anti-immigration sentiment. The schema underlying this discourse is the belief that there are rules for immigration, codified in law, that should be followed. If an immigrant fails to follow these rules, they are viewed as illegitimate or "bad." If an immigrant follows these rules, they are viewed as legitimate or "good." People use this conventional discourse to negotiate the boundaries of what counts as legitimate immigration, and we find that it is used by conservatives and liberals alike. A key feature of this discourse is that it articulates a rational, empirical difference between "legal" and "illegal" immigration, and pathways to citizenship for some immigrants who arrive in the country illegally.

While it is not always explicit, race plays a central role in the *immigration requires rules* discourse. Often people evoked symbols like Ellis Island (as Anna did above) to signify a wave of immigration, primarily from Europe, of people who are now generally considered white. For people like Anna, these immigrants followed the rules and are therefore legal, legitimate immigrants. This invocation of "legitimate" historical European immigration is often contrasted with images of immigrants crossing bodies of water or physical barriers at the southern border–immigrants who fail to follow the rules. While it is almost never made explicit, this distinction between legal and illegal immigration (and the implicit distinction between the types of people who engage in each) racially codes these symbolic statements and others like them.

Anna combined *immigration requires rules* with *national security* when she said: "They had rules. If you had disease or you had something that was going to potentially harm the people here, they didn't let you in." In this excerpt, Anna used the *national security* discourse to justify why *immigration requires rules*. Anna did not use any first-person pronouns here, though, subtly distancing herself from being the one to judge whether someone should be allowed to immigrate to the United States – "they" (the rule-making body, the government) made that decision. This is different from the previous conventional discourse, where she noted "we" were letting in "bad people." However, there are some similarities: Both conventional discourses attempt to make sense of how and when an immigrant should be "let in." Here, the target of Anna's frustration is the immigrant who poses a threat when protective rules are not in place or not enforced.

The third conventional discourse, the *humanitarian* discourse, is used to express pro-immigrant sentiment; it the most decidedly pro-immigrant of the three conventional discourses discussed here. The schema underlying this discourse is the belief that immigrants, documented or not, are people who are entitled to rights and should be treated with compassion. It is most frequently evoked by liberals; unsurprisingly, it does not appear in our conversation with Anna and Leo. However, it did appear in many of our interviews across the political spectrum. Aliya, a young Muslim woman and leftist activist living in Milwaukee, used this discourse to counter Trump's immigration policies when speaking to an imagined supporter of those policies: "You support families being torn apart. You support mothers being taken away from their ... babies taken from their mothers." In this excerpt, Aliya accentuates the harm done by Trump's immigration policies, using phrases like "torn apart" and "taken away." She repeatedly uses second-person pronouns ("you") to frame Trump supporters as complicit in these actions, and the present progressive verb "being" emphasizes that these actions are ongoing. Talk about family separation is a common feature of this discourse, with many framing this separation as inherently compassionless. Often, the target of frustration is people who support President Trump's immigration policies, but this discourse can also be used to express frustration toward politicians and policies perceived as devaluing immigrant lives.

4.1.1 Immigration Discourse In-Person and on Twitter

There are stark differences in how people use these conventional discourses in interviews and how they use them on social media platforms, particularly Twitter. In the interview, Anna oscillates between anti-immigrant and occasional pro-immigrant sentiments, stringing together *national security* and *immigration requires rules* conventional discourses while also allowing space for certain forms of immigration. These seemingly contradictory conventional discourses were often present among our interviews, and they were not seen as being "at odds" with one another in many conversations (Strauss, 2012). *Immigration requires rules*, in particular, provides people with space to negotiate the conditions under which immigration can be either "good" or "bad." This discursive space for negotiation within conversations tended to mediate even the strongest anti-immigrant viewpoints.

Unsurprisingly, we do not observe this phenomenon in Twitter discourse. We know that Twitter tends to attract people who are more politically engaged and tends to encourage more extreme, hostile, and reductive discourse (Mellon and Prosser, 2017). Although the *immigration requires rules* discourse allowed some space for negotiation in our interviews, this discourse looks very different on Twitter. Tweets from two conservative Twitter users provide an illustration:

> Only gullible (dumb) college students call illegal immigrants "dreamers." Grow up, they're criminals who want 2 steal what U have & ruin it.

> @WashTimes @SpeakerRyan no amnesty for any illegal aliens including DACA and anchor babies. No more taxpayer money for illegals. DACA people are illegal. Not our fault. No more $$$$$

Unlike the interviews, where even the staunchest of conservatives could employ seemingly contradictory conventional discourses, creating the possibility of discursive negotiation, Twitter discourse distilled the logic of the conventional discourses to their most reductive, uncompromising, and extreme forms. We saw this reductiveness and polarization in Twitter discourse around all three of our key issues; this is a key difference between conventional discourse in conversations and on social media.

There are a number of potential explanations for this phenomenon. First, the situational context greatly alters the linguistic form of each discourse. Notably, the interviews ranged from 30 minutes to 3 hours, giving participants ample time to discuss their views on immigration and other political issues, while Twitter limits users to 280 written characters. Naturally, there is more space in interviews and in everyday life to express contradictory views or propose a more nuanced perspective of complex political issues.

A second factor may be the nature of the communication. Interviewers aimed to create an open environment for conversation, often interviewing people in natural groups where there were preexisting relationships. This openness and familiarity likely helped limit adversarial tendencies in political conversation. By contrast, Twitter is a digital, public platform that limits certain discursive responses (e.g. indicating that you are listening to a person), which may produce a more combative discourse exchange.

4.2 Immigration Discourse in the Communication Ecology

Next, we explore the dynamics of the communication ecology using our time-series models. Figure 7 illustrates the relationships between different media platforms, specifically, national news, discourse by and about national elites and local actors on Twitter, local newspapers, Google search volume, and general Twitter. Figure 7 summarizes the relationships observed across thirty-two Prais-Winsten regressions in Appendix 5, Table 1_1 to Table 1_32. Additional illustrations summarizing the key relationships among aspects of the communication ecology are contained in Appendix 6 (https://mcrc.journalism.wisc.edu /battleground-appendices/).

First, we find that national news media share coverage patterns across the political spectrum and across the three framing devices – *national security, immigration requires rules*, and *humanitarian*. That is, national news media across the political spectrum (left, right, and center) use all three conventional discourses about immigration, albeit to different degrees; this suggests that these discourses are generally isolated from one another, but actively produce content. However, when we examine the proportion of the framing devices used by national news sources, it becomes clear that conservative frames dominate in both conservative *and* moderate news. In fact, more than 80 percent of the framing devices surrounding immigration on the right and center are related to the overwhelmingly anti-immigrant *national security* discourse. The fact that this conservative, anti-immigrant

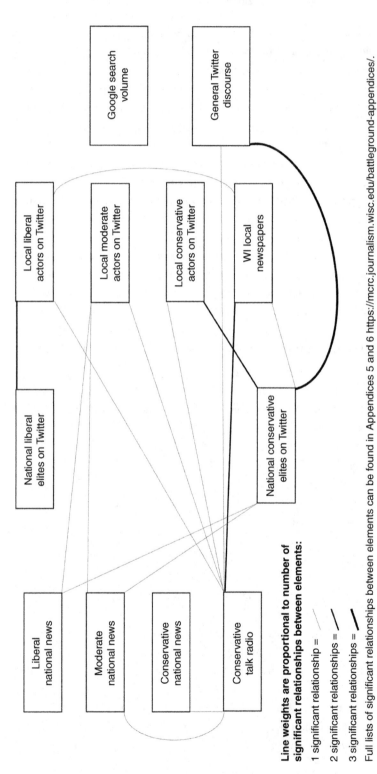

Line weights are proportional to number of significant relationships between elements:

1 significant relationship =

2 significant relationships =

3 significant relationships =

Full lists of significant relationships between elements can be found in Appendices 5 and 6 https://mcrc.journalism.wisc.edu/battleground-appendices/.

Figure 7 Partisan discourse flow in the media ecology (immigration)

frame dominates in moderate national news coverage as well as conservative coverage suggests that conservative media has more discursive power on issues of immigration.

Second, we find that the conservative media ecosystem has an outsized relationship with nonelite Twitter discourse related to immigration. We found that with all three conventional frames for the immigration issue, the discourse used by and surrounding conservative national Twitter elites was associated with general Twitter users' use of those same discourse frames. For example, when discourse surrounding conservative national elites on Twitter emphasizes the *immigration requires rules* discourse, other Twitter users discussing the topic employ more of that same discourse. The same pattern follows for *humanitarian* and *national security* discourses, suggestive of some discourse control by conservative elites.

We found that talk radio plays a particularly central role in the conservative media ecosystem on immigration-related discourse and frames. Talk radio's use of immigration frames co-occurs with immigration discourse surrounding local Twitter actors across the political spectrum, but it also predicts general Twitter discourse. This highlights the importance of talk radio not only to the conservative ecosystem but to the rest of the media ecology. Parsing the role of talk radio in shaping the overall media ecology, particularly on the political right but also across the ideological spectrum, is an area of research that demands much more attention.

Third, there are two discourse-specific trends worth noting for our theoretical interests. We find that Wisconsin newspapers are responsive to the *humanitarian* discourse surrounding national conservative Twitter elites and local liberal Twitter actors. One reason for this may be that stories about the Wisconsin dairy industry are prevalent in our newspaper data. The resonance of the *humanitarian* discourse in the state and its prevalence in Wisconsin newspapers signals that, although immigration tends to be a more nationalized issue, there are still meaningful connections between immigration and the daily life of many people across Wisconsin: Immigrant labor is essential to Wisconsin's dairy and other agricultural industries.

We also find that the *immigration requires rules* discourse and frame devices across the media ecology related strongly with discourse surrounding national conservative elites and local conservative actors on Twitter (see Appendix 6). Our deeper qualitative analysis of these tweets revealed that many Twitter users employed this specific discourse to make anti-immigrant claims. Some of these tweets discussed legal immigration pathways (Deferred Action for Childhood Arrivals policy [DACA], in particular) but broadly rejected their validity. While we found that, in conversation, the *immigration requires rules* conventional discourse can facilitate conservative acceptance of some immigration policies, Twitter discourse is far less nuanced; conservative elites' anti-immigrant use of this discourse on Twitter can effectively chip away at the legitimacy of even legal immigration policies like DACA.

Our time-series analysis makes the asymmetric nature of discursive power surrounding immigration visible. Conservative frame devices dominated not only conservative national news but also moderate national news. The use of immigration discourse surrounding conservative elites on Twitter co-occurs with the same type of discourse in nonelite Twitter. Finally, talk radio immigration frame devices co-occur with similar discourse surrounding local Twitter actors across the political spectrum and general Twitter discourse. Immigration appears to be an issue that is effectively "owned" by conservatives, who have more discursive power in the media ecology during conversations about immigration. The question remains whether this translates into the ability to shape public opinion on restrictive immigration policies.

4.3 Multilevel Modeling of Immigration Public Opinion

Using 2018 survey data focusing on representative Wisconsin residents, we employ multilevel models to enhance our understanding of how social position, local context, and media flows shape public opinion on immigration (see Appendix 7 for methodological details, and Tables A_1 to A_3 for the full HLM models for immigration opinion). We specifically focus on Wisconsinites' attitudes toward a restrictive immigration policy (1 = oppose, 5 = favor; M = 3.26, SD = 1.39). Overall, our models show that about 33.6% of variance of the immigration policy position is explained by demographics and party identification, an additional 4.7% by media exposure and communication patterns, and about 0.3% by socioeconomic changes in local county-level contexts.[6]

Individual demographics and news use patterns have a dominant influence on people's positions related to immigration. We find that people who are older, male, less educated, and Republican are more likely to favor a restrictive immigration policy. While the individual-level demographic factors account for the majority of variance in our models, we do find that there are significant relationships between media and communication patterns and individuals' attitudes about immigration policy. In general, our findings highlight the role of national news media in shaping attitudes about immigration; we find no effect of local news or social media. These findings align with the theory of

---

[6] This is calculated using conditional R2 of multilevel models, which refers to variance of the outcome variable explained by the entire model, including both fixed and random effects (Nakagawa et al., 2017)

nationalization, as the influence of national news eclipses the influence of local news or local information networks related to immigration. However, other findings complicate this picture. Notably, our findings show that political talking-partners and local economic conditions also shape immigration attitudes: although news media influences are nationalized, people still seem to interpret immigration through the lens of daily life and social interactions (i.e. the lifeworld).

We also find that estimated exposure to *national security* and *immigration requires rules* frame devices through national conservative media and talk radio is associated with more support for restrictive immigration policy, while exposure to these same frame devices through liberal or moderate media is associated with *less* support for restrictive immigration policy. These opposing outcomes suggest that platforms play a key role in the effect of frame devices. One explanation for this is that the ideology of a news source shapes how it packages and deploys frame devices. For example, liberal media may use *national security* frames in order to critique them, potentially inoculating viewers against conservative uses of this frame. Conservative media may use *immigration requires rules* as a way of critiquing or exposing flaws in the current immigration system, similar to what we saw on Twitter. This highlights the importance of national news and platform ideology in shaping public opinion, as well as the importance of analyzing context through careful qualitative analysis to make sense of these broader trends.

Despite the critical role of national news and platform ideology, people's context and daily life still serve as a lens through which they make sense of immigration policy. Having at least one Republican discussion partner is associated with increased support for restrictive immigration policies. This is a common finding throughout the rest of the empirical sections and underscores the important role of political talk in shaping and understanding public opinion. Similarly, we find that local economic conditions shape public opinion on immigration. People living in counties where manufacturing jobs increased are less likely to support restrictive immigration policies, while people living in counties that have lost manufacturing jobs are more likely to support restrictive immigration policies (see Figure 8).

When we examine the interaction between the local economy and people's partisan identity, we see a polarizing effect of immigration on public opinion. When county-level employment conditions improve, we see the gap between Democrats and Republicans grow, as Republicans become more supportive of restrictive immigration policies while Democrats become less supportive of these policies (see Figure 9). High unemployment counties show a smaller gap in these partisan preferences. Our results confirm patterns that have been found in previous work (Suk et al., 2020), in which partisans show more polarized attitudes in

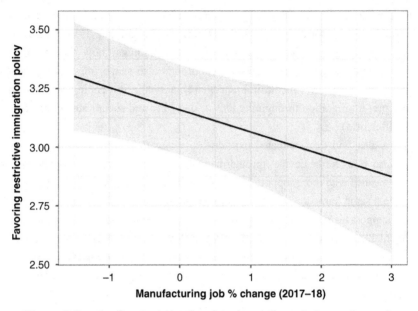

Figure 8 Support for restrictive immigration policy relative to change in manufacturing jobs at the county level

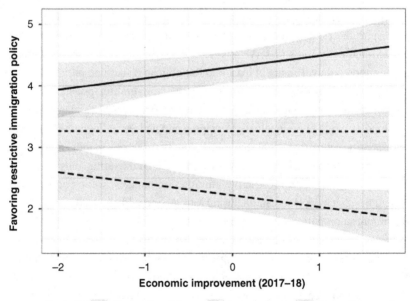

Figure 9 Support for restrictive immigration policy relative to improving economic conditions at the county level and individual partisanship

counties with superior or improving contextual conditions. It is possible that individuals with contextual deprivation are more interdependent and less motivated to pay attention to politics (Solt, 2008), while those with contextual prosperity retreat to their political camps to secure their social advantage.

4.4 Conclusion

Our analysis reveals the potential power of the nationalization of immigration discourse. In general, discursive power surrounding immigration was centered around national media outlets and actors. Most notably, in the media ecology, conservative actors had considerable discursive power: Conservative elites (on Twitter), national conservative outlets and conservative talk radio, and conservative frame devices (e.g. *national security*) dominated media flows. Immigration is an issue often owned and dominated by conservative politicians and their rhetoric. Our findings on the media ecology have allowed us to examine the aggregate-level patterns of asymmetrical discourse power centered on conservatives surrounding the issue of immigration.

We also found that there were important differences in how people used immigration conventional discourses in interviews versus social media. In interviews, participants often used conservative discourses such as *immigration requires rules* to allow for the possibility of legitimate immigration. However, this was not the case on Twitter. Twitter users talking about or to conservative Twitter elites often used the *immigration requires rules* discourse with the *national security* discourse to delegitimate even legal immigration processes. On Twitter, immigration discourse is in its most extreme, distilled form, while in conversation even staunch conservatives engage in more nuanced, contradictory immigration discourse. These differences in the quality of discourses in-person and on Twitter were consistent across all three cases.

It is also notable that immigration discourse flows in the media ecology are indeed related to public opinion formation about immigration policy. Our approach allowed us to look at how relative framing exposure through different media sources produced a more nuanced, complex understanding of immigration policy than the black-and-white views often expressed on Twitter. Generally, we find a robust effect of national media – liberal, moderate, and conservative – on immigration policy attitudes, and an equally robust effect of conservative talk radio and conservative talk networks. Interestingly, we did not find that local news media and local social media had this kind of discursive power. However, we find that overall, Wisconsinites' understanding of immigration is more complicated than is presented by the nationalized media ecology. The nationalization effect occurs alongside geographic economic conditions indicated by unemployment rates and the availability of manufacturing jobs. In other words, people make sense of immigration through a synthesis of national news information and their lifeworld.

5 Healthcare: A National Issue with Lifeworld Implications

with Sadie Dempsey (*University of Wisconsin–Madison*), Jiyoun Suk (*University of Connecticut*), Josephine Lukito (*University of Texas–Austin*), and Ellie Yang (*University of Wisconsin–Madison*)

Thomas and Levi settled into their well-worn recliners inside an auto shop on the corner of two long stretches of county highway in rural Wisconsin. Chickens clucked and rustled their feathers in a cage on the floor nearby. Both men worked as loggers for decades. Thomas is in his eighties and long retired. Levi is in his fifties and left logging to work in lawn care, his leathery skin evidence of countless long days spent in the sun. Philip walks into the auto shop from the dusty junkyard out front to join in the conversation, standing close by with his hands folded across his chest. Now in his sixties, Philip grew up on a farm not far from the auto shop and spent time working as a cross-country trucker before landing his current job as a contractor. The men were comfortable together after spending many, many mornings in this very spot, helping themselves to coffee while talking about the news of the day. Thomas is a vocal Trump supporter, but Levi and Philip's political leanings were harder to pin down, as they regularly critiqued both political parties, and politics in general. When the conversation turned to healthcare, all three men had strong opinions informed by their own experiences as independent contractors living in rural Wisconsin.

Thomas: I'm a retired logger. I'm on social security. It takes over $200 of my wife's and my checks for Medicare. Besides that, we're paying a $400 supplement plan. So, we're paying over $600 a month.

Levi: That 'bamacare is a joke. Some plans, you've got to pay $6,000 upfront, $400 each day you're in the hospital. . . . Some people are paying $12,000. . . . There's no way. I can't afford it.

Philip: Our choices were severely limited. Right now, Midwest Clinic is pretty much monopolizing healthcare in the area. They will only accept two insurance plans. . . . I'm not happy with that. I see this big business just eating the public alive. They pretty much have a monopoly. They're protected by laws that . . . They're the healthcare. The old lady down by the river can't treat somebody.

Throughout the conversation about healthcare, Thomas, Levi, and Philip drew largely from their personal experiences with insurance. These same types of intimate anecdotes appeared in most of our interviews, with teachers, students, and retirees like Thomas all talking about their struggles and the failures of the contemporary American healthcare system. Grievances about the cost of healthcare were especially prevalent in these interviews.

In many ways, discourse surrounding healthcare is distinct from the other topics we studied. When people discussed their experiences with healthcare, they relied heavily on their personal experiences in the lifeworld – specifically, their interactions with the healthcare system. This is quite different from the other two cases we study here – immigration and Foxconn; people varied greatly in their direct experience with those issues, whose impact might depend on one's social position or geographic location. But everyone has been impacted by the healthcare system; in 2019, about 92 percent of Wisconsinites had health insurance coverage.

When talking about their experience with the healthcare system, people focused almost exclusively on negative experiences. Because people had largely negative experiences with healthcare, it was impossible to divide conventional discourse about healthcare into pro- or anti-healthcare discourses. Moreover, it is impossible to categorize these conventional discourses as distinctly liberal or conservative. While there were partisan-aligned immigration and Foxconn discourses, the healthcare discourses were extraordinarily similar across the ideological spectrum.

However, this does not mean that healthcare discourse transcends partisanship. We see the influence of ideology emerge when we examine how people attribute blame for their healthcare grievances. Democrats tend to blame Republican elites or corporate greed in the healthcare industry. By contrast, Republicans tend to blame government influence broadly or Democratic elites specifically for the healthcare crisis. People with less strong partisan attachments, like Levi and Philip, borrow from one or both of these critiques. For example, Levi adopts a more conservative critique by blaming Obamacare for the high cost of healthcare, while Philip adopts a more leftist critique by centering blame on the greed of the insurance industry.

In this section, we delve more deeply into the conventional discourses on healthcare that we observed across interviews and look for traces of these on Twitter and in the frame devices favored on news media. First, we examine three conventional discourses concerning healthcare and their corresponding media frames. Second, we use time-series analysis to look at the flows of these discourses and frames across social media and news platforms over time. Our analysis suggests that in the realm of healthcare, the left enjoys more discursive power. Third, we use multilevel modeling to examine how exposure to these conventional discourses in media shapes public opinion about Obamacare (Affordable Care Act). We find that local economic conditions and political talk in daily life influences public opinion related to healthcare.

5.1 Healthcare Conventional Discourses

As with all of our cases, there is a broad range of conventional discourses people use when talking about healthcare. We narrowed our focus to the three that are most prevalent across our data layers: (1) *healthcare is overpriced* (2) *big money in healthcare* (3) *vulnerable populations*. As noted above, these could not simply be divided into pro- or anti-Obamacare positions, because they each highlight a distinct critique of the healthcare system. Instead, we focus on tracking these conventional discourses based on rhetoric and the underlying schema.

Healthcare is overpriced is seemingly the most straightforward. The underlying schema is that many people are unable to afford insurance or medical care; that when people can afford insurance, the quality of insurance is so poor that it is not worth the cost; and that the costs associated with healthcare are unjust. When this conventional discourse is deployed, two dominant and distinct entities are blamed for the high cost of insurance. For some people, more often those on the left, the high cost of insurance is attributed to corporate greed on the part of the insurance companies or healthcare providers. For others, more often those on the right, the high cost of insurance is due to government incompetence; this variation is most often used by conservatives to critique the Affordable Care Act. However, these different attributions of blame are not mutually exclusive.

Thomas, Levi, and Philip all used this conventional discourse. Thomas used his own life experience to illustrate how healthcare is too expensive for him and his wife; this use of personal anecdotes to illustrate this conventional discourse was common across our interviews. Levi leveled a critique against Obamacare specifically, highlighting how government intervention failed to make healthcare affordable for the average person. Philip attributed blame for high insurance costs to corporate greed, claiming that he sees "this big business just eating the public alive." However, Philip sees the government as also partly to blame; he also said that the health insurance industry is "protected by laws," and therefore, by the state. As this illustrates, this conventional discourse is often used within a populist framing. *Healthcare is overpriced* highlights the way that economic or political elites (whether greedy corporate overlords, the state, or a combination of the two) prevent everyday people from accessing affordable, quality healthcare.

Big money in healthcare is another frequently occurring conventional discourse. The underlying schema is that politicians are "bought" by economic elites, particularly the health insurance and pharmaceutical industries (sometimes colloquially referred to as "big pharma"); rather than representing the interests of constituents, politicians represent corporate interests and their own self-interest. While this conventional discourse is most often used by those on the left to critique the Republican Party, it is also used by the right to critique the Democratic Party, and by both liberals and conservatives to criticize the corruption of politicians in broader terms. This discourse is often used alongside others, like *healthcare is overpriced*, but it can also stand on its own. *Big money in healthcare* is tied specifically to the idea that the healthcare system is flawed because of the influence of political special interests.

The last conventional discourse, *vulnerable populations*, is humanitarian in nature. The underlying schema is that there are particular groups of people who are vulnerable and require government intervention to ensure they have access to care. Vulnerable groups include veterans, children, the poor, the elderly, and those with preexisting conditions. Thomas, for example, tapped into this conventional discourse when referring to the fact that he is on Social Security and his wife is on Medicare, implying that their old age makes the high price of healthcare even more egregious. This conventional discourse was particularly prominent in our Twitter discourse layer.

5.2 Healthcare Discourse in the Communication Ecology

Our time-series analysis reveals a partisan asymmetry in healthcare discourse across Wisconsin's communication ecology. Figure 10 summarizes healthcare discourse flows based on thirty Prais-Winsten regressions (see Appendix 5, Table 2_1 to Table 2_30, https://mcrc.journalism.wisc.edu/battleground-appendices/). Just as immigration shows a clear asymmetry favoring conservative media, we find that liberal media is particularly influential in shaping healthcare discourse. This suggests that discursive power is largely issue dependent, and likely indicates that there is partisan "ownership" of discourse in particular issue areas. Just as Republicans have come to increasingly "own" immigration in public perception, healthcare has become a central pillar of the Democratic platform and political campaigns.

As in the previous section, we did not focus on the relationship between each set of conventional discourses and frame devices, instead attending to the broader patterns of associations to gauge constellations of relationships among social and news media. This approach allowed us to see the centrality of liberal national news to the healthcare discourse, and to track its resonance

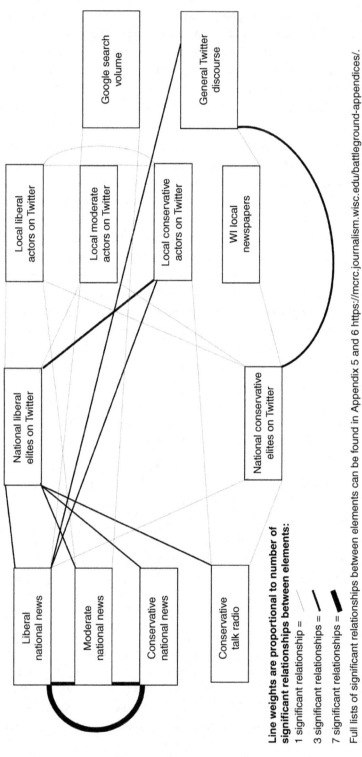

Line weights are proportional to number of significant relationships between elements:

1 significant relationship =

3 significant relationships =

7 significant relationships =

Full lists of significant relationships between elements can be found in Appendix 5 and 6 https://mcrc.journalism.wisc.edu/battleground-appendices/.

Figure 10 Partisan discourse flows in the media ecology (healthcare)

across other data layers. We found that when liberal news media increased their critical framing of healthcare, so did moderate and conservative national news outlets. Liberal news critiques of healthcare are also associated with the volume of conventional discourses concerning healthcare among Twitter elites at national level and political actors at the local level (especially conservative actors). In other words, when national liberal outlets emphasize the three healthcare frames, the Twitter discourse surrounding partisan elites at the national level and political actors at the local level also center problems concerning healthcare, as does the Twitter discourse concerning healthcare among general Twitter users. In the case of healthcare, therefore, liberal national news plays a major role in Wisconsin's statewide media ecology.

Senator Tammy Baldwin, the only Wisconsin national liberal elite in our Twitter sample, also plays a central role in healthcare discourse: When the discourse surrounding her concerns conventional discourses about healthcare, we also see similar discourses about healthcare cropping up among local Twitter actors across the political spectrum. However, while Tammy Baldwin is more consequential for discourse surrounding local actors on Twitter, only national conservative Twitter elites have an effect on the broader healthcare discourse on Twitter.

This time-series analysis revealed the central role that national liberal news plays in shaping discourse on healthcare across the Wisconsin communication ecology. Particularly at the national news level, we see a partisan asymmetry suggesting that liberal media enjoy more discursive power than conservative media around this issue. However, the role of discourse on Twitter appears mixed. Our evidence suggests that, at the elite level, conversations about healthcare surrounding liberal elites may have more influence than those surrounding their conservative counterparts. At the level of general discourse, however, it appears that conversations about healthcare surrounding conservative elites may have more influence; this again suggests an asymmetry of influence. There is still work to be done to parse the role of partisan influence within the Twittersphere with respect to healthcare (see Appendix 6, https://mcrc.journalism.wisc.edu/battleground-appendices/).

Second, we found that discourse on healthcare involving local conservative Twitter actors tends to increase with discourse on healthcare surrounding Tammy Baldwin. By contrast, liberal and moderate Twitter actors at the local level tend to respond to a wider range of national news and Twitter elites. This suggests that on the topic of healthcare, liberal national Twitter elites have somewhat more power to shape discourse than conservative national Twitter elites, especially among local Twitter actors across the ideological spectrum.

However, our findings suggest that conservative national Twitter elites are the only group that has a significant role in shaping *general* Twitter discourse surrounding healthcare in Wisconsin. This suggests that while liberal news outlets, in particular, have some ability to shape discourse surrounding healthcare across all our data layers, conservative elite Twitter discourse continues to have an outsized association with general Twitter discourse on this issue.

5.3 Multilevel Modeling of Healthcare Public Opinion

Our multilevel modeling reveals the importance of county-level social contexts and lifeworld experiences in shaping public opinion on healthcare. In modeling public opinion, we specifically focused on attitudes about Obamacare, one of the most polarized healthcare policies in America. In the survey, we asked respondents the extent to which they favor Obamacare (1 = oppose, 5 = favor; M = 3.1, SD = 1.59). Appendix 7 contains methodological details of these models, with Table 2_A to Table 2_C presenting the full HLM models for healthcare opinion (https://mcrc.journalism.wisc.edu /battleground-appendices/). Overall, our multilevel models suggest that about 46.4% of variance of the Obamacare issue position is explained by demographics and party identification, an additional 4.1% by media exposure and communication patterns, and about 0.2% by socioeconomic changes in local county-level contexts.[7] As with most models concerned with human behavior, individual-level factors account for most of the variance in these models. However, these multilevel models allow us to capture important variation attributable to media and communication patterns as well as local factors.

Exposure to healthcare coverage through partisan media outlets has unsurprising effects. Exposure to healthcare frames through liberal and moderate media sources is positively associated with favoring Obamacare while exposure to healthcare frames in conservative media and conservative talk radio is negatively associated with favoring Obamacare. We also observe that healthcare frames flowing through local media coverage and healthcare discourses encountered on Twitter appear to be positively associated with Obamacare favorability. This is distinct from immigration, where we saw no influence

---

[7] This is calculated using conditional R2 of multilevel models, which refers to variance of the outcome variable explained by the entire model including both fixed and random effects (Nakagawa et al., 2017).

from local news or social media. This finding suggests that healthcare may be somewhat less nationalized than immigration with respect to the influence of media.

However, we observe important effects when we include interaction effects between partisan identity and estimated exposure to healthcare frames through different media outlets in our model (see Figure 11). First, we see significant negative interactions between party identity and exposure to conservative-leaning outlets, including national conservative partisan media and conservative talk radio. Democrats who are exposed to healthcare frames through conservative media and conservative talk radio are less likely to favor Obamacare; Republican support for Obamacare remains low regardless of healthcare frame exposure through these same outlets. This trend is mirrored when examining exposure to healthcare frames through liberal or moderate media: Republicans' support for Obamacare increases when exposed to healthcare frames through liberal or moderate media, while support among Democrats remains high. We also see a similar pattern for social media. This signals to us that it is the partisan lean of the sources of discourse that is most consequential for shifts in public opinion related to healthcare.

Our models also highlight the importance of interpersonal talk in shaping opinions about healthcare. We show that having at least one Republican discussion talk partner is related to negative attitudes toward Obamacare (see Figure 12). In other words, when people talk to Republicans about politics, they are less likely to support Obamacare. This shows that political talk – just one small part of people's lifeworld – can be consequential in shaping opinions on political issues. This makes sense, because we know that discussions with others is one of the central ways people make sense of politics and formulate opinions.

We further show that local economic conditions shape the effects of political talk. In counties where unemployment rates dropped, political talk about healthcare has a polarizing effect. Improvements in employment conditions are associated with less support for Obamacare among people with Republican talk partners and more support for Obamacare among people without Republican talk partners. In other words, improved local conditions appear to exacerbate existing individual preferences linked to the diversity of individuals' political talk networks. Consistent with Suk et al. (2020), we see evidence that people in economically well-off and resourceful communities may retreat to politically polarized positions depending on their political talk partners. Taken together, these findings reflect the importance of local context and lifeworld, particularly talk networks, in shaping

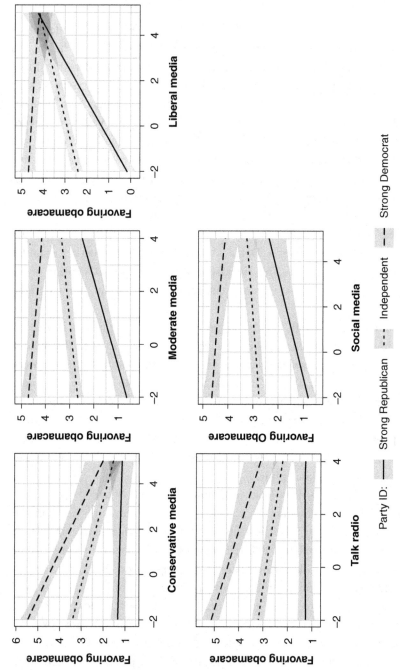

Figure 11 Support for Obamacare by party identity and media exposure

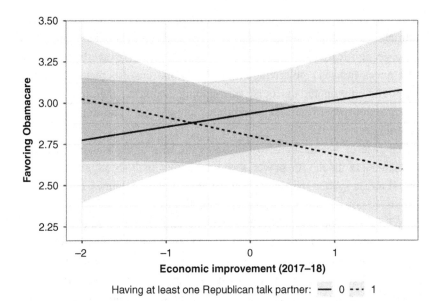

Figure 12 Support for Obamacare by economic improvement (2017–18) and Republican talk partner

public opinion about healthcare. While county-level unemployment conditions are just one way of operationalizing a small aspect of a much more expansive lifeworld, the interaction between local economic conditions and political talk highlights the urgent need for models of public opinion to incorporate local context and lived experience.

5.4 Conclusion

Our analysis reveals the importance of lifeworld and social context to understanding public opinion surrounding healthcare. In our interviews, people often used their everyday lives as a lens for making sense of healthcare policy. Thomas, the retired logger discussed at the beginning of this section, used his own experience with Medicare to illustrate that even with government assistance, healthcare was simply too expensive for him and his wife. Philip used his experience with the local clinic to explain how the healthcare industry is to blame for outrageous healthcare costs, while Levi used his knowledge of other people's experiences to blame Obamacare and the government. We know from our multilevel models that political talk –the same type of talk that Thomas, Philip, and Levi engage in every day– is critical for public opinion formation. Having just one Republican talk partner, like Thomas, is associated with lower support for Obamacare. We also know that local economic conditions are particularly consequential for how political talk shapes these opinions. As local labor market conditions improve, political talk across the partisan divide tends to exacerbate partisan differences and has a polarizing effect. All of this suggests that understanding public opinion and discourse surrounding healthcare requires an understanding not only of national conditions, but of local conditions and lived experiences as well.

The case of healthcare also illustrates the role of issue ownership and asymmetry in discursive power. Our time-series analysis suggests that the liberal media system, particularly at the level of national news, enjoys more discursive power than the conservative media system on the issue of healthcare. This is the opposite of what we saw in immigration, where the conservative media system was dominant in shaping discourse. These two cases together suggest that media system-level perceptions of issue ownership may play a role in determining when and how asymmetries in discursive power are present. However, it is important to consider the qualitative differences in healthcare and immigration. In immigration, the discourses were relatively easy to divide along partisan lines, while this was nearly impossible to do with healthcare. This invites the question: What does it mean to enjoy discursive power when the discourse being influenced isn't clearly aligned with a particular political agenda? Examining the differences between issues "owned" by Democrats and Republicans may prove an interesting area of future research. Expanding our universe of cases could help us see whether this pattern is more general: Does discourse surrounding issues owned by Republicans tend to be clearly divided along partisan lines while discourse surrounding issues owned by Democrats tends to be less so? If this is the case, it could suggest another qualitative dimension to discursive power that is centered on how the *type* of discourse can enhance or reduce discursive power.

6 Foxconn and Economic Development in the Local Communication Ecology

with Josephine Lukito (*University of Texas–Austin*), Sadie Dempsey (*University of Wisconsin–Madison*), Jiyoun Suk (*University of Connecticut*), and Jordan M. Foley (*Washington State University*)

As Gary sits down, he promptly discloses that he considers himself an expert in all things political. Although his bushy gray mustache partially obscures a broad smile, he is only half-joking. Gary is a semiretired businessman from the Fox Valley who loves keeping up with political news. His mornings start early with the news program Fox & Friends at 5 a.m. and he continually checks the news throughout the rest of the day. Gary is a longtime Republican, an early and enthusiastic Trump supporter, and considers Scott Walker to be the "greatest thing that has ever happened to this state." Gary cares deeply about national and state-level politics and pays close attention to the news. However, when asked about Foxconn – a Taiwanese electronics manufacturer that negotiated a $3–4 billion deal with the Walker administration to build a plant in Racine county – Gary gave an uncharacteristically hesitant response.

Gary: I certainly back it [Foxconn]. But it's so big and so out there that it's hard to even fathom. Something that all businesspeople really struggle with now is finding employees. Everybody that I talk to goes, "Where are they going to find these 10,000 employees?" . . . It's so vast that it's really hard. I don't have real strong opinions for or against. . . . Even if I don't get any work out of it, it may tie up some of my competitors; that will make it easier for me to get other jobs. I'm for any construction. But I really don't have a strong opinion on Foxconn other than I'm for it. . . . It's just economic growth. . . . Even though we're giving them tax . . . the residual effect of that, the way it trickles to other businesses, suppliers, right down to who they hire to cut the grass. Because I guarantee you, they won't have their own people cutting the grass. . . . It definitely has a positive effect on the economy. There's no doubt about it. It's going to drive wages up, you know?

Gary's account of Foxconn is hardly straightforward. He begins by expressing his support for the manufacturer, but hedges his opinions by describing the deal as too large for him "to even fathom." He brings in knowledge that he hears from others ("everybody that I talk to") to make sense of the deal's limitations – primarily the problem of finding a workforce. While Gary says he supports job creation, he and the other business owners we interviewed consistently talked about how difficult it is to find workers for their businesses. They cannot fathom how Foxconn will find workers to fill the 13,000 jobs it originally promised, and they are concerned that Foxconn may strain the state economy. As he talks through his ideas about the Foxconn deal, Gary considers how his business would benefit from it, describing his support as "obvious." By this point, he has transitioned from doubt to a neutral-to-positive stance. When pushed on the question, Gary ultimately falls in line as a Republican and a Walker supporter, making a broader argument about how it would benefit the broader economy, thus relying heavily on the logic of trickle-down economics to justify his support for Foxconn.

Gary is not unique – political opinions are far from perfectly constrained or consistent. This is especially true when discussing policy about economic development, which often encompasses international, national, state-level, and local dynamics simultaneously, requiring an ability to balance benefits and costs both for oneself and for one's community. This invariably leads to contradictory conclusions that require reconciliation.

In this section, we analyze discourses in conversation and social media and corresponding frame devices in news coverage, linking these to public opinion about Wisconsin's Foxconn deal. While we explored other discourse about economic development (the original issue we set out to study), we found that messages about Foxconn specifically dominated the corpora. The Foxconn deal serves as an excellent exemplar of a local economic development policy that has garnered national attention, and we therefore focus here on this as a case study of media influence on political opinion at both the national and the local level.

Like many states, Wisconsin has seen its economy transformed over the past fifty years, due in large part to increased globalization and technological developments. Concerns about the health of the economy, the rising cost of goods, and the loss of well-paying jobs preoccupy the thoughts of millions of US citizens. It is under these conditions that then Governor Scott Walker negotiated the Foxconn deal, which promised to bring 13,000 jobs to Wisconsin in exchange for a $3 billion tax incentives package – the largest US incentive ever offered to a foreign company. The appeal of the deal was the potential to bring in thousands of manufacturing jobs to the state economy; in Wisconsin, manufacturing still accounts for nearly 20 percent of gross state product, and it employs almost 16 percent of the Wisconsin workforce (see National Association of Manufacturers, n.d.). In fact, Wisconsin is one of many states to offer targeted economic development subsidies to bring foreign and domestic tech companies to the state in the hope of "creating jobs." Despite how common these deals are, research has shown that they tend to underperform, and do not bring about regional growth in either tech or manufacturing industries (see Mitchell et al., 2020; Peters and Fisher 2004).

Our analysis of the discourse surrounding the Foxconn deal reveals key partisan arguments regarding the value of incentive-based economic development policy. Compared to the discourse identified for the immigration and healthcare issues, the discourses we identified around Foxconn were highly evaluative and aligned (unsurprisingly) with participants' respective party positions. We observed a highly engaged media ecosystem that includes interactions between news and social media, liberal and conservative media, and national and local media; our modeling of the public opinion data shows that the consumption of certain Foxconn frame devices through partisan media could shape attitudes about Foxconn, more closely aligning them with the position being communicated.

6.1 Foxconn Conventional Discourses

Drawing from our interview data, we analyzed four conventional discourses that emerged as the most prominently used by our participants: (1) *Foxconn is too expensive*, (2) *Foxconn is bad for the environment*, (3) *Foxconn is not American*, and (4) *Foxconn is good for the economy*. Unlike any of our other cases, the Foxconn conventional discourses are clearly divisible into pro-Foxconn and anti-Foxconn discourses. As the above excerpt from Gary's interview shows, even people who clearly identify themselves as being on one side or the other of the Foxconn debate use both pro- and anti-Foxconn discourses in interviews, and they sometimes braid these discourses together. Governor Scott Walker (unsurprisingly) played a prominent role in all the conventional discourses around Foxconn, because of his position in leading and promoting the creation of the Foxconn incentives package.

Foxconn is too expensive is the most prevalent anti-Foxconn conventional discourse across our data layers. The schema that underlies this discourse is that the potential benefits of bringing Foxconn to Wisconsin will never justify the cost of the incentive package. On both the left and the right, this is often accompanied by a discussion of opportunity costs: Many note that the incentives given to Foxconn could have been used instead to support Wisconsin businesses.

Gary exemplifies two key ways in which right-leaning individuals tend to use this discourse. First, he talked about the sheer size of the deal ("it's so big ... that it's hard to even fathom"). Concern about the high cost of the tax incentives was common in our interviews, even among Republicans like Gary. Second, he expressed doubt about whether there would be enough people to take the jobs ("Where are they going to find these 10,000 employees?"). This concern was particularly acute among conservatives and business owners we spoke with, who lamented their own difficulty in finding quality employees.

Left-leaning individuals who use this discourse frequently describe the incentives as a form of corporate welfare, highlighting a perceived Republican hypocrisy: These critiques point out that arguing against limited government intervention in the form of a social safety net contradicts advocacy for government to provide a massive tax incentive package. When these discourses were used by left-leaning people, they often made puns with the word "con" (e.g. "Foxconn'ed"), evoking the idea that a gullible mark was being tricked out of money, in this case, Republicans and Foxconn working to defraud taxpayers.

Another anti-Foxconn conventional discourse is *Foxconn is bad for the environment*. This discourse focuses on the potential detrimental environmental impacts of the Foxconn plant on Lake Michigan, specifically, and on air quality and other bodies of water more broadly. This conventional discourse taps into the schema that the environment is an important public good for a wide variety of reasons – innate value, recreation, tourism, hunting, agriculture – and that it must be protected. In our interviews, people on the left and on the right used this conventional discourse alongside discussion of the importance of Wisconsin's natural resources. Maria, a young Latina living in Milwaukee, used this discourse during a broader discussion of environmental racism, pointing out that the natural environment must be protected in order to safeguard local people. She said, "Lake Michigan is being dumped into by Foxconn . . . and nobody's really up in arms about that just because of the fact that Milwaukee is pretty minority heavy. It just feels it's kind of being ignored while our water's being polluted."

The final anti-Foxconn conventional discourse we consider is *Foxconn is not American*. Building on previous conventional discourses, this rhetoric focuses on Foxconn as a foreign company. Messages using this conventional discourse often highlight Foxconn's Taiwanese or Chinese origins, make references to communism, or simply describe the company as "not American." This discourse taps into a schema relying on a form of zero-sum logic, claiming that the interests of America and its citizens should be prioritized over those of other countries and noncitizens. Under this schema, providing an incentives package to Foxconn drains resources away from American citizens or American companies. One particular example used was the Kimberly-Clark paper mill in Wisconsin's Fox Valley, which was threatening plant closures around the same time that Foxconn was being subsidized to open its plant. This conventional discourse tends to have a nationalist quality. While it is primarily used by those on the right to critique Foxconn, it is also used by those on the left.

Cathy, an administrator living in a Milwaukee suburb who identifies as a Democrat, explained her feelings toward Foxconn:

> One of the big things is the giveaway to Foxconn. I think it's absolutely horrendous that the state gave that company the incentive package that it did. Now . . . oh, I can't think of the company up in the Fox River Valley. One of the paper mills. They're saying, "Okay. You've done this for a company that, a foreign company that has no presence in Wisconsin. We've been here for decades now. We want a corporate handout."

Foxconn is good for the economy is the sole pro-Foxconn discourse we include in our analysis. This conventional discourse centers around both the direct and the indirect economic benefits offered by the Foxconn deal – most prominently, the creation of jobs. The schema that underlies this conventional discourse is grounded in the assumption that increasing manufacturing and high-tech jobs is *a* way (if not *the* way) to improve the economy and generate economic growth. It is worth noting that the original incentives package focused on the direct benefits of creating employment in manufacturing, which is essential to the Wisconsin economy. The indirect benefits that supporters see rely on the logic of trickle-down economics and include everything from ripple effects through the supply chain to the indirect creation of jobs by supporting restaurants and services needed by the influx of new residents.

Gary focused heavily on these indirect, trickle-down effects of Foxconn, which he believes will be good for the economy as a whole and thus good for his own business. In an egotropic way, he referenced how Foxconn might benefit his construction business ("Even if I don't get any work out of it, it may tie up some of my competitors; that will make it easier for me to get other jobs"). In a more sociotropic way, he referred to the benefits Foxconn may offer to the state as a whole, across multiple different industries ("it trickles to other businesses, suppliers, right down to who they hire to cut the grass").

6.2 Foxconn Discourse in the Communication Ecology

As with previous sections, we now turn to our time-series modeling to examine how these discourses flowed between media platforms. Discourse flows concerning Foxconn are illustrated in Figure 13, which summarizes forty-three Prais-Winsten regressions found in Appendix 5, Table 3_1 to Table 3_43. As with the immigration and healthcare discourses, news outlets were highly reactive to one another when discussing Foxconn. One major reason for this is the way that Foxconn was covered in both national and local news media: Stories about the deal used both pro-Foxconn arguments and anti-Foxconn arguments in attempts to provide a "balanced" portrayal of the policy (see Appendix 6, https://mcrc.journalism.wisc.edu/battleground-appendices/).

Our findings highlight the important role of talk radio in the media ecology in discussions of Foxconn. On Twitter, the Foxconn discourses that were used in and around the accounts of local moderate actors and national conservative elites shared the frame devices that were evoked in talk radio coverage and commentary concerning the deal. However, the shifts in discourse that talk radio evoked may not have been intentional, unlike with other issues: Talk radio uses more anti-Foxconn discourse

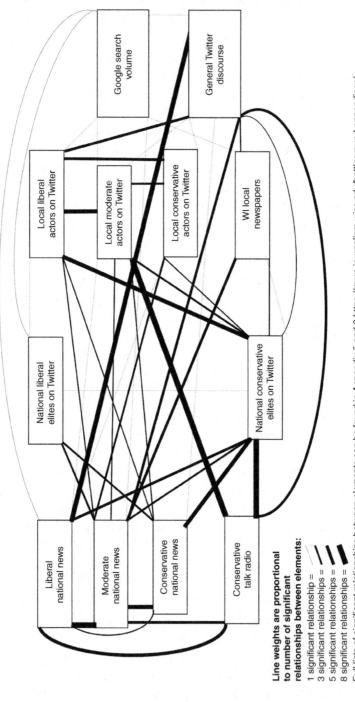

**Line weights are proportional
to number of significant
relationships between elements:**

1 significant relationship =
3 significant relationships =
5 significant relationships =
8 significant relationships =

Full lists of significant relationships between elements can be found in Appendix 5 and 6 https://mcrc.journalism.wisc.edu/battleground-appendices/.

Figure 13 Partisan discourse flows in the media ecology (Foxcomm)

(Foxconn is too expensive, Foxconn is bad for the environment, Foxconn is not American), but the other platforms simply tended to use fewer pro-Foxconn discourses (with the exception of moderate media). While we found that talk radio use of Foxconn discourses paralleled increases in volume across other media layers, our results also show that talk radio may be discussing the issue differently from other platforms, even partisan-aligned platforms. Notably, there are far more exchanges on Foxconn discourses – both pro- and anti-Foxconn – between conservative national Twitter elites, conservative national news, and talk radio than between their liberal or moderate counterparts. This suggests that the conservative media ecosystem is more tightly bounded than liberal or moderate media ecosystems in its coverage of Foxconn.

Wisconsin newspapers appeared to be especially attentive to anti-Foxconn discourse from moderate national news outlets. When moderate national news used more *Foxconn is too expensive* and *Foxconn is bad for the environment* frame devices, Wisconsin newspapers used more anti-Foxconn frame devices – both these two devices and the *Foxconn is not American* device. While our other data layers tend to be deeply interconnected, Wisconsin newspapers stand out in that they are almost solely related to one source – moderate national news. In contrast, general Twitter discourse about Foxconn was tightly bound with national liberal news framing and, to a lesser degree, local liberal actors on Twitter.

Relative to the other topics studied, discourse about Foxconn was more connected across multiple media layers, with frequency of content increasing at both the national and the state level at the same time. However, these media layers did not necessarily use the same discourses at the same time. For example, when liberal national news used anti-Foxconn frames like *Foxconn is too expensive*, general Twitter used more pro-Foxconn discourse, like *Foxconn is good for the economy*. Similar patterns were found with moderate and conservative national news, and talk radio (see Appendix 6).

6.3 Multilevel Modeling of Economic Evaluations

We now turn to our multilevel modeling to examine how exposure to discourses about the Foxconn development and state economy related to Wisconsinites' evaluations of their economy. As in the other sections, we use multilevel modeling to test how shifts in socioeconomic conditions at the county level, individual demographics, and communication patterns combined with frame dominance are simultaneously related to evaluations of the

Wisconsin economy. Appendix 7 contains the methodological details model; Table 3_A and Table 3_B show the full HLM models for opinion about the Wisconsin economy (https://mcrc.journalism.wisc.edu/battleground-appendices/). We specifically focus on retrospective evaluations of the state economy: Respondents assessed Wisconsin's economic status *over the past year.* About 38% (N = 779) felt that the state economy had improved during that time; about 22% (N = 468) felt that the state economy had got worse; and about 33% (N = 690) believed that it stayed about the same. According to our models, about 37.8% of variance of the economic perception is explained by demographics and party identification, 3.6% by media exposure and communication patterns, and around an additional 2% by socioeconomic changes in local county-level features (though no individual factors were significant). In general, we show that none of the county-level features are related to the retrospective evaluations of the state economy, but our analysis of media and communication patterns perhaps revealed the most interesting information.[8]

We first test how positive assessment of the economy – the opinion that the state economy has got better – relates to several factors: people's demographics, their exposure to economy discourses through specific media sources, and their political talk patterns. Controlling for county-level contextual shifts over the past year, we show that people who are older, male, educated, Republicans, and have higher income are more likely to believe that the state economy has improved. We also found that the partisan slant of people's media sources affected how they retroactively evaluated the state economy. People who were exposed to a preponderance of supportive frame devices through conservative media (emphasis on devices like *Foxconn is good for the economy* over *Foxconn is bad for the economy, Foxconn is not American,* and *Foxconn is bad for the environment[9]*) had a higher probability of evaluating the state economy as having improved. However, exposure to the same frames through nonconservative media outlets or sources (liberal media, moderate media, Twitter, local media) remains insignificant. Finally, we found that having at least one Republican discussion partner is also associated with positive retrospective economic evaluation.

In sum, it is not only demographics that affect economic evaluations. We see a strong association between communication patterns and economic

---

[8] This is calculated using conditional R2 of multilevel models, which refers to variance of the outcome variable explained by the entire model, including both fixed and random effects (Nakagawa et al., 2017)

[9] We identified this as a conventional discourse, but it was not used as often as the four we discuss in detail here.

evaluations: The more people are exposed to supportive frames via conservative media sources, or the more people engage with conversations with at least one Republican, the more likely they are to assess the state economy positively. It is also noteworthy that exposure to the same frames through liberal or moderate national media, Twitter, or local media remains insignificant. This confirms the critical role of conservative media in the media ecology around economic discourse more broadly and Foxconn discourse specifically. Controlling for contextual shifts in their counties, partisans (both conservatives and liberals) who have higher conservative media consumption in general feel that the state economy has improved in the last year, while those with lower conservative media use are less likely to believe this (see Figure 14 [c]). Strong Republicans (thick line) with the lowest level of conservative media use still have about a 75 percent probability of saying that the economy has got better, while strong Democrats with the lowest exposure to conservative media had a very low probability of seeing economic improvement, just below 5 percent. Democrats with the highest exposure to conservative media were almost as likely to believe that the economy had improved as Republicans with the lowest exposure to conservative media, with about a 70 percent probability of holding this belief.

Interesting patterns also emerge for liberal and moderate media sources. For strong Democrats, the probability of positive economic evaluations remains generally low regardless of the dosage of exposure to liberal and moderate media. However, both conservatives and liberals who are highly exposed to partisan media from the opposite end of the political spectrum show the most drastic difference in their economic opinions: While partisans' views toward the state economy are largely polarized along party lines regardless of their level of pro-attitudinal media consumption, exposure to counter-attitudinal media shapes evaluations of the economy.

We also found that exposure to supportive frame devices over critical ones operated differently through liberal and moderate media than exposure to relative framing of Foxconn benefits via conservative media. Overall, partisans *highly exposed* to Foxconn framing devices *via liberal and moderate media* are less likely to indicate the state economy has got better than those who are exposed to those framing devices via conversative outlets (see Figure 14 [a] and [b]). This may be because liberal and moderate outlets emphasize critical aspects of the Foxconn deal more than the possible benefits in their framing, or that the political slant of the medium through which these frames are delivered can shape people's opinions.

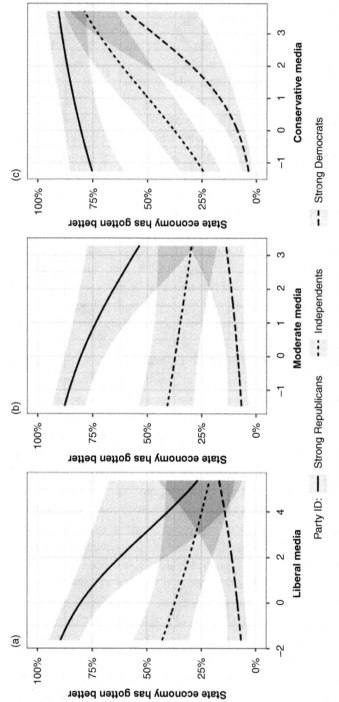

Figure 14 Economic evaluations by party identity and media exposure

6.4 Conclusion

Strategically communicating about the economy is one of the most important issues across most elections. Politicians seek to attribute positive economic growth to themselves and to lay the blame for economic recessions on their opponents (Vavreck, 2009). As campaign strategist Carville said during Bill Clinton's 1992 Presidential run, "it's the economy, stupid." The results of our analysis show that people's perceptions of the economy, and of economic policies such as the incentives used to attract Foxconn, are shaped by a combination of media influences, geographic context, and how people link contextual change to their lived experience.

Unsurprisingly, people who identified as conservative were particularly responsive to pro-Foxconn frames and to discourse about how Republicans are good for the economy. This makes sense, as the narrative promoted by Governor Scott Walker and other local and national conservatives emphasized the Reaganesque economic logic that economic gains from the deal would "trickle down" throughout the state economy.

However, it was surprising that consumption of conservative media content was more powerful in shaping Foxconn public opinion attitudes among conservatives than liberal media was at shaping attitudes among liberals. Such findings suggest that there is an infrastructure for maintaining issue ownership – which relies on news coverage and social media discourse to disseminate discourses that align with a party's economic policy – and that conservative media infrastructure is stronger and more effective than liberal or moderate media infrastructure, at least for this issue. We saw the effects of these large-scale influences in the discussion with Gary, reported at the beginning of the section. Despite the fact that he was exposed to anti-Foxconn discourse from people he talked to (and used some of these anti-Foxconn discourses himself, alongside the pro-Foxconn discourses he repeated), he still ultimately aligned with his party in supporting the Foxconn deal.

7 Understanding Communication Ecologies in Asymmetric Media Systems

Our examination of the dynamics of Wisconsin's political communication ecology shows the complexity of the interactions among national and local news coverage, social media conversation, elite messaging, interpersonal talk, and local contextual dynamics; these all work together to shape opinions about immigration, health care, and the economy. In this section, we synthesize the major findings of our Element. We focus on insights about the interactions among the components of the communication ecology across five major domains:

(a) the nationalization of US politics;
(b) partisan asymmetry in communication flows;
(c) issue ownership and discursive power;
(d) contextual effects on opinion; and
(e) how conventional discourses and framing devices move across conversation, social media, and news media within this increasingly hybrid media system.

In this section, we also articulate an agenda for future inquiry, calling for complex investigations that integrate multiple data collection and analytic strategies in order to help us understand democracy in our contentious times, during a period of media hybridity and asymmetry.

7.1 Nationalization

While we found evidence to support the nationalization thesis of American politics (Hopkins, 2018) in our Wisconsin analyses, our results also reveal the importance of state-level news ecologies, social media flows, and political conversation networks. In other words, political media is indeed a fully interconnected ecology: state-, local-, and individual-level communication layers interact with the national layers and with each other, shaping and being shaped by the discourses and attitudes used in multiple outlets within and across other levels. For example, we saw that in the immigration issue, discursive power surrounding immigration was generally centered around national media outlets and actors, and national news use was associated with immigration opinions. But with the healthcare issue, we saw that national issues can also be influenced by local information flows. For instance, frame devices in liberal national news co-occurred with healthcare conventional discourses used by Twitter elites at both the local and national level, as well as by those retweeting, replying to, and mentioning these elites. At the local level, the use of local news was associated with changes in attitudes about the Affordable Care Act. And the Foxconn issue, which is largely a state rather than a national issue, became nationalized to some degree by President Trump giving it attention; this shaped the national focus in mass media and social media conversation.

Despite the importance of national news flows and national elite conversations on social media across these issues, our analyses revealed that nationalization is complicated by local political conversation. Individuals' local talk partners were consistently correlated with opinion formation with respect to the issues we studied. Moreover, our qualitative analyses revealed that the conventional discourses used when talking about politics reflected local issues and experiences – that is, the lifeworlds of citizens coming in contact with these broader national issues. Although there are ways in which American politics is nationalizing, the central features of people's everyday life and engagement with politics are decidedly local.

7.2 Partisan Asymmetry in Communication Flows

Our analysis aligns with and extends the past decade of scholarship highlighting partisan asymmetries in the US political system, showing how issues, platforms, and frame devices work in ways that disrupt prior notions of partisan balance. Our work found that partisan asymmetries were persistent, but that the degree and nature of asymmetries varied across issues. For instance, in the Foxconn case, we found evidence of greater issue dualism – the tendency to divide an issue debate into contending pro and con perspectives – in discourses and news. With the immigration issue, conservative messages (unsurprisingly) dominated conservative national news, but they also dominated moderate national news as well as talk radio, whose immigration frame devices co-occurred with what local Twitter elites and nonelite Twitter users were tweeting about.

What might help explain the asymmetric dominance on the topic of immigration? In addition to our qualitative interviews with more than 200 Wisconsin citizens, we talked to a few dozen political and media elites, including the powerful and prominent former conservative radio talk show host Charlie Sykes (interview with Charlie Sykes, 2017). According to Sykes, Republican Governor Scott Walker had consistently been the politician most willing to appear on talk radio, from when he worked at Milwaukee County Executive; by the time he was governor, Walker was regularly strategizing messaging off-air with Sykes, leading to coordinated communication on-air. The coordinating power of political talk radio on the right demands more attention.

Just as a conservative asymmetry was evident on immigration, liberal asymmetry was apparent on the issue of healthcare. Although elite liberal operatives do not have the affordances of talk radio in the way that conservatives do, they are still able to dominate discourse flows about healthcare, especially on Twitter; this suggests that discursive power may be dependent on partisan issue ownership (Fagan, 2021). It is also notable that conservatives' *discursive power* around immigration was mainly limited to the Wisconsin political communication ecology, while influence on *public opinion* was limited to national media players; in contrast, liberals' discursive power around healthcare extended to public opinion, where national and local media use were linked with (positive) attitudes about the Affordable Care Act.

This raises questions of issue ownership and local vs. national discursive power, borne out by our analysis of the Marquette Law School Poll, whose cross-sectional longitudinal surveys of Wisconsin adults offer a broader perspective; we were able investigate changes in immigration and healthcare attitudes across different local contexts over time. The data in Figure 15 show that public opinion change on immigration was consistent across regions, becoming more favorable to a progressive immigration policy over time, though this shift stalled out somewhat during the 2016 to 2018 period and around the midterm election. Healthcare saw much more dramatic regional shifts in opinion, with liberals seeming to win the opinion battle in two Republican strongholds, the suburban ring of WOW counties and rural areas, as seen in Figure 16. This might be explained by the interplay of contextual factors, media use, and talk and social media networks (see Appendix 8 for details of the opinion polls, https://mcrc.journalism.wisc.edu/battleground-appendices/).

7.3 Issue Ownership

The evidence we present here is consistent with the idea of "issue ownership," or the public belief that one major political party is better able to handle a particular issue than the other major party (Petrocik, 1996). Immigration is seemingly owned by Republicans, and healthcare appears to be owned by Democrats, yet everyday political talk about these "owned" issues used heterogenous conventional discourses, showing that even issues that tend to be owned by one party can be considered in a nuanced way that does not always follow the party line (Zaller, 1992). As our qualitative interviews showed, partisans often say that they are wholly in alignment with their party's position on some issue, yet at the same time raise considerations that problematize or even contradict that position. The nuance on display in interpersonal communication does not appear in news and social media discussion flows, where people stake out more strident positions along partisan lines. This could be one reason why media, at both the national and the local level, tend to reflect conservative talking points on immigration and liberal talking points on healthcare: The parties "own" these issues, and the conventional discourses and frames that nonpartisan media deploy reflect the broadly partisan control of how these issues are discussed.

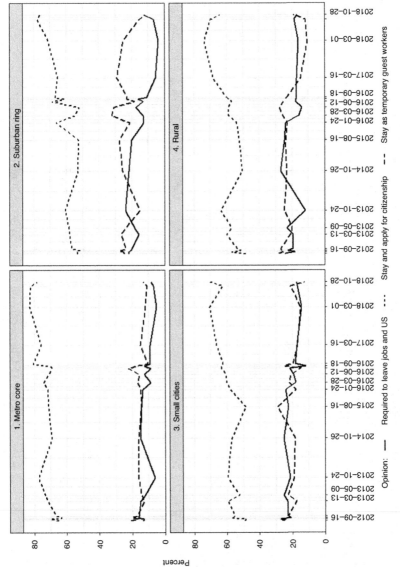

Figure 15 Immigration opinion by Wisconsin region

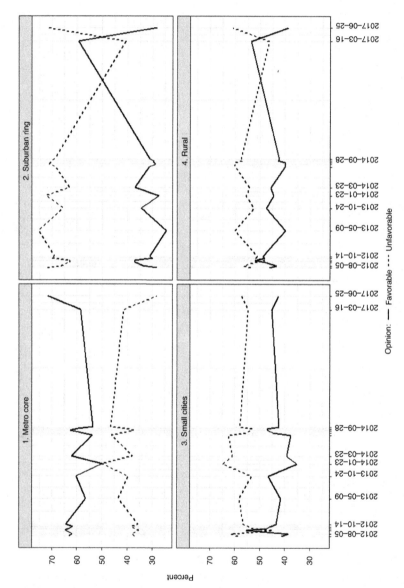

Figure 16 Obamacare opinion by Wisconsin region

The conventional discourses on these two issues were not purely ideological as people also talked about how the issues intersected with their own lifeworld experiences, but, broadly speaking, the Twitter and news coverage of each issue tended to use the same type of frame devices preferred by their party. As Wagner and Gruszczynski (2016) have shown, Republicans tend to frame issues more symbolically and Democrats tend to frame issues in terms of operational policy solutions.[10]

However, our Foxconn analysis did not reveal ownership by either party, per se, at least initially. We found that for a performance issue like the economy, conventional discourses were organized in more pro–con terms: conventional discourses were either positive toward Foxconn and its economic prospects or negative about Foxconn and its environmental and social impact. In other words, discourse around Foxconn did not fall neatly along party lines; people talked about the issue in ways that were difficult to classify as either full support for, or serious opposition to, the Foxconn plant deal. Most people used conventional discourses from both the pro- and anti-Foxconn positions. Uniquely, Foxconn was both a state and a national issue, driven by executives rather than arising from citizens: Governor Walker led the charge on the issue in the state, and President Trump jumped on board, touting the deal on Twitter and even going to Wisconsin to claim credit for it. The Foxconn case thus highlights how an issue that is less commonly considered to be owned by one party can become partisan.

Our findings are consistent with recent work showing that "ownership" may be too strong a word for the parties relationship with issues – rather, they may have short-term leases on issues and our conventional discourse and Twitter analyses provide a path to studying how these leases can break down or be strengthened. Just as Darmstra et al. (2021) show that there are relevant preconditions for issue ownership in contested multiparty systems, our work suggests that similar battles are waged at different levels in overlapping media ecologies.

7.4 Contextual Effects on Opinion

Social context can exacerbate or mitigate polarized partisan attitudes (Suk et al., 2020). In this Element, we have provided evidence for the relationship of opinion to changing social contexts; specifically, county-level changes over a one-year period in unemployment levels, population aging, and health

---

[10] As Ellis and Stimson (2012) put it, Americans' preferences are symbolically conservative but operationally liberal.

outcomes. We found that when context affects opinion, it does so in ways that are consistent with prevailing theories: As conditions improve, political preferences tend to harden and polarize, and when conditions worsen, preferences tend to become less polarized, as citizens look to a wider range of political options to solve pressing problems.

When county-level employment conditions improved, the gap between Democratic and Republican preferences grew, with Republicans expressing more support for restrictive immigration policies, and Democrats doing the opposite. Conversely, high unemployment was associated with the weakening of these partisan preferences. Similarly, we found that improved local conditions exacerbate existing partisan preferences linked to the homogeneity of individuals' political talk networks; improvements in employment conditions were associated with less support for Obamacare among people with Republican talk partners, but with more support for Obamacare among people with Democratic talk partners. Public opinion about healthcare, and, specifically, the Affordable Care Act, is related to local context and to lifeworlds, particularly talk networks. Although contextual factors did not shape economic opinion, talk networks did, with Republican talk partners linked to positive economic evaluations.

Of course, changes in county-level unemployment conditions are just one small way of operationalizing an element of the contextual social structure. In the future, social context might be studied more thoroughly by examining changes in local conditions over longer periods of time, or changes at different contextual levels; studies might also incorporate other ecological factors, such as the robustness of the news ecology, voting behavior, manufacturing labor, educational attainment, and county demographic change. We return to potential avenues for future research in Section 7.7.

7.5 Conventional Discourses and Communication Flows

Each empirical section (Sections 4, 5, and 6) began with a summary example of the hundreds of interviews we have conducted across the state of Wisconsin over the past six years. These vignettes showcased how Wisconsin citizens used rich, varied, and sometimes ideologically contradictory conventional discourses to make sense of major political issues affecting their lives, their community, the state, and the nation more generally. We showed that these conventional discourses also appear in social media discussion and news coverage of the same issues, but we found that conversation on Twitter and frame devices in the news relied upon more ideological, polarized expressions, which were both more strident and less varied than those used in the conversations we had with

Wisconsinites. These differences make sense, as conversation inherently allows for more complexity and nuance than other types of media: Twitter has strict character limits, and news media relies on traditional structures of storytelling and framing.

Despite the limited, rather threadbare uses of conventional discourses on social media, the social media conversations by elites and citizens remain important, as journalists are heavy users of social media, relying on it to gauge sentiment and using it for conversations that shape their reporting. Indeed, some use tweets as newsworthy exemplars of public opinion in their news coverage (McGregor, 2019; McGregor and Molyneux, 2020, Wells et al., 2016).

This has implications for our understanding of contentious politics in the information ecology of a single state. Although Twitter may shape journalistic coverage, it is decidedly not representative of public opinion. The conversations people have about political issues in real life are far more heterogeneous – and, critically, more ambivalent (Alvarez and Brehm, 2002) – than is seen on social media. This may be partly because the frame devices that make their way into news coverage are associated with partisan asymmetries, as noted above. Future research might explore how the conventional discourses in media and news coverage compare with those used in conversation networks in terms of their power to shape political opinion.

7.6 A More Comprehensive Communication Ecological Approach

For the past decade, we have been studying the role of political talk, social media flows, news flows, and social contexts in opinion formation and political and civic participation. The work we have reported in this Element is a first cut into what is possible when our approach – the integration of multiple data sets, multiple research methods, and multiple layers of analysis – is applied comprehensively. We intend that our future research will expand on the theoretical and analytic framework we have outlined here, examining questions of communication ecologies and communication flows within the increasingly asymmetric and polarized hybrid media system that we observed. Going forward, we aim to expand our analytic frame, both temporally and contextually.

The analysis and summaries we provide above omit as much as they include. We hope that our future research will address this by expanding our data collection and integration efforts; we plan to include campaign advertising content and placement, more comprehensive local broadcast media content, a wider range of statewide newspapers, and the local conservative talk radio programs that are so central to residents' day-to-day media experiences. We also plan to expand social media collection beyond Twitter, harvesting public-facing content from platforms like Facebook and Instagram and forums such as Reddit and Tumblr. We collected additional swing state panel studies during the 2020 election, and, at the time of writing, we are planning to repeat this in 2021 and 2022; this will allow for even deeper media data integration and the development of change models that consider dynamics across elections. All of this is on top of expanding our current collections and collaborations with additional in-depth interviews and more waves of the Marquette Law School Poll (MLSP) survey, as well as adding archives of legislative activity and campaign fundraising.

We present this broader data map in Figure 17. This expanded map has a number of features that merit attention. First, it is important to note that the data sources are arrayed by contextual level, starting with the national and the statewide, then moving to the regional level (or designated market area representing a zone of dominant media influence), and then to the county and community/precinct level. This attention to multilevel context is of considerable import, given that individuals are nested within these varying contexts. Second, the temporal frame is extended to 2024, indicating the need to look beyond a single election cycle or even a two-year window (like the one that this Element addresses). We plan to extend our timescale and to use a data analytic framework such as MONOCAR (Tahk, 2015, see also http:// monocar.tahk.us/), which will allow for the type of interrupted and noisy time-series modeling required to tackle these longer time dynamics. Third, and most subtly, is the expansion of the contextual data to include hundreds of contextual factors at multiple social levels. With these additions, the data structure we propose for our ongoing study of the Wisconsin communication ecology includes the following elements:

- Data from the Wesleyan Media Project (formerly, Wisconsin Advertising Project), which has tracked the placement, content, and tone of political ads reaching Wisconsin residents since 2008.
- Semi-structured interviews, expanded to include more than 300 residents across the state.
- Additional interviews with Wisconsin media and political elites from both the Republican and the Democratic parties.
- Retrieved content from forty national news outlets, spanning national legacy, broadcast, and digital media, including partisan sources and conservative talk radio.

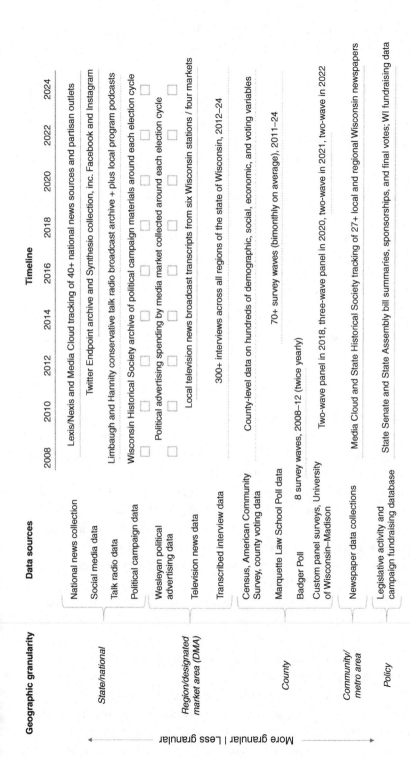

Figure 17 Expanded data map of Wisconsin communication ecology components

- Over 100,000 archived stories from 27 Wisconsin newspapers as well as broadcast transcripts from 6 local TV news stations spanning 4 major Wisconsin markets.
- Public-facing social media content concerning Wisconsin politics from 2016 onward, including archival access to a 10 percent sample of Twitter content, all relevant Reddit and Tumblr content, and all relevant public-facing Facebook and Instagram posts.
- Over seventy waves of the Marquette University Law School poll of state-wide opinion.
- Three more custom panel surveys of Wisconsin residents in 2020, 2021, and 2022.
- Country-level contextual data on hundreds of demographic, social, and economic factors.
- All legislative activity (including bill summaries) and campaign fundraising databases.

Figure 17 emphasizes our continued attention to the ways that social media and news discourses shift over time as they exist alongside contextual changes in demographic, social, economic, and voting characteristics.

7.7 Future Directions

We have already begun collecting and assembling data for this expanded data framework; this opens many new possibilities for analysis, as does our expanding methodological toolkit, which we plan to apply to both the new data and the data we have previously assembled. Moving forward, we will do more comprehensive comparative case analyses like the immigration, health-care, and Foxconn cases we have compared here. We aim to expand these future cases to include additional issues, election and nonelection contexts, and a broader tracking of media content and usage for multilevel modeling. We are doing this already for projects on vaccine hesitancy and election fraud beliefs around the 2020 US presidential election and its aftermath. For these projects, we build on our work presented here, tracking news and social media discourses across a wide range of sources and platforms, then integrating these content data into our multiwave panel data collections to gauge whether specific communication flows reaching individual respondents appear to shape their attitudes.

Our large-scale time-series modeling approach, which estimates over 100 models, allows us to examine the robustness of discursive power relationships without getting bogged down in each specific discourse. However, this approach means that there is less attention to the relative power of specific discourses. Future work may expand each of the empirical sections in this Element (Sections 4, 5, and 6) to consider those differences, exploring whether certain conventional discourses and frame devices have greater discursive power than others. Examining these questions in the context of the 2020 presidential election would further reveal the limits of our conclusions and their potential generalizability.

Two important directions for our future work include greater attention to the roles played by Facebook and by local broadcast media in Wisconsin's communication ecology. In our 2018 and 2020 panel surveys, we asked a variety of questions about local television news use and use of Facebook as a news source and found that both were among the most widely consumed sources for local political news, substantially exceeding Twitter. Ignoring these sources in discussions of the state's communication ecology (and by extension, the national ecology) is a real problem that must be corrected.

Therefore, for our future work, we have begun drawing keyword-queried content from Facebook and Instagram via Synthesio, just as we did for Twitter in the current project. We have also begun using CrowdTangle, a Facebook public insights tool, to launch related projects centered on specific Facebook pages. For example, we are using CrowdTangle to gather public posts from county-level Democratic and Republican Party pages about major topics such as election fraud. We hope this will help us to understand how local partisan elite claims about the election were interpreted by Facebook users and to discover how these same messages flow outward to other platforms and in local news coverage. By matching these data with our Synthesio database, we can analyze information flows on Twitter, YouTube, Reddit, and other major platforms.

In terms of local broadcast media, we are expanding our focus to include transcripts of local news broadcasts, largely because local TV news remains the main source of news for Wisconsinites (as it is for most Americans). More and more of the state's stations are now owned by Sinclair Broadcasting Group, which is known to centralize control of local news operations to emphasize conservative political perspectives (Martin and McCrain, 2019). Other local broadcast content with a conservative slant includes hundreds of hours of conservative talk radio content shared on radio stations throughout the state. National conservative talkers Rush Limbaugh and Sean Hannity have had large clearances in Wisconsin, and the state has had a large crop of local conservative talkers (previously Sykes, and still Belling and McKenna, among others) who dominate rural and suburban airwaves. Local talk radio pervades the state and amplifies both national and state conservative talk (Cramer, forthcoming).

We are also applying computational text mining techniques like structural topic modeling and semantic network analysis that may be helpful in unearthing additional insights from our qualitative interview data. We have 228 interviews and counting, systematically collected from residents throughout the state, purposively chosen to reflect a range of views, experiences, and identities. We plan to add at least 70 more in the coming years; with 300+ interviews, this will be one of the largest in-depth interview datasets we are aware of in the realm of state-level politics and political communication. We will include covariates in our topic modeling work, such as partisanship, age, gender, occupation, and region of residence; these will help reveal differences in themes that emerge from different groups. Combining this with semantic network analysis or analysis of topic model networks (ANTMN), which have already been used to detect frames in news texts, may reveal additional sets of conventional discourses (Walter and Ophir, 2019). Our expanded data collection makes these extensions of our current work possible.

8 Conclusion

It was a curious correspondence of theoretical interest and practical events that led our team to focus on the state of Wisconsin as an empirical case for the study of political communication. The 2011 protests in Madison against Act 10 – the Capitol's occupation by anti-Walker protesters, a rally headlined by Sarah Palin, street theatrics, and the Forward Marching Band –were only a fifteen-minute walk away from our offices at the university, located at the other end of State Street. Our friends, colleagues, students, and family members were involved in various aspects, and on various sides, of the conversation and activism that took place at the time and in the following years. And the fallout could affect people's livelihoods: The contentiousness of the petition drive to recall Governor Walker made the relatively innocuous choice to sign a petition a perilous one, as the names of all signatories were made public.

Being so close to this controversial activity heightened our awareness of how intensely local and interpersonal politics is, even in the twenty-first century – even as we saw protests being organized over social media and national media descending on the state. We were already investigating the broader dynamics of the hybrid media system (Wells et al., 2016) and reflecting on Cramer's (2016) revealing study of the importance of place in organizing citizens' understandings of politics. When Wisconsin unexpectedly swung to Trump in 2016, it crystallized our interest in how the local and personal intersect with the networked and mediated.

This Element is thus an early attempt to understand how citizens make sense of the political world through the *combination* of their local and interpersonal experience, their consumption of national-level political media, and everything in between. We have pursued a model of political communication that can accommodate both citizens' realities in specific, real places and the networked "nationalized" media that exists abstractly, in the space of flows (Castells, 2010). Our effort is in the spirit of Chadwick's (2017) call for "both-and" approaches that can accommodate the complex dynamics of how citizens now understand their world. We extend Chadwick's account of media hybridity, which simply sought to integrate broadcast and digital media logics; we seek to integrate the *macro* levels at which we conceptualize communication flows with the *local* communication dynamics and contextual factors of people's everyday lifeworlds.

Having sketched the results of our several investigations into these dynamics, we conclude by revisiting some of the theoretical questions and propositions that began the Element, focusing particularly on the questions that political communication can work to answer more fully.

There is clearly a great deal more to do to describe the complex interplay of the components described by our model. We have only begun to understand, for example, how narrative frames in media interact with conventional discourses; we still have not fully explored the extent to which citizens draw on media depictions when they verbally make sense of their political (or economic, or cultural) situations. Such questions have significant ramifications for understanding the influence of media, such as talk radio, that appear highly influential despite relatively modest audience sizes. Is it the case that discourses propounded by talk radio reach much larger numbers of people than their audience numbers would imply, through repetition in everyday conversation? The echoes of Katz and Lazarsfeld (1955) here are very clear, but how true does their thesis remain eighty years after their investigations, in a radically different media climate? To what extent do interpersonal interactions take place outside of face-to-face contact – over social media or private messaging apps such as WhatsApp? What kinds of discourses, and what kinds of media, enjoy this sort of travel?

Finally, as the reader will have noted, this theoretical project requires significant innovation in methodological tools to enable the analysis of multiple layers of meaning-making. The conceptual tools of conventional discourses (Strauss, 2012) and discursive power (Jungherr et al., 2020) have been invaluable in enabling us to move between the interpersonal discursive contexts that reflect citizens' everyday interpretive frameworks and the various layers of social and news media discourse in which those ideas are reflected and re-presented. Text-processing tools have enabled us to characterize large quantitative collections of texts and organize them into time-series datasets, and survey research has allowed us to compare the contributions of social-structural position, local community changes, and news media experiences in multilevel models exploring citizens' opinions on key issues. In all these cases, it has been a pleasure to learn from colleagues working in related areas. As we continue this line of exploration, we recognize that reconstructing the political communication ecology in its full complexity must be a collaborative effort, one that we hope to have advanced here.

References

Abernathy, P. M. (2018) *The Expanding News Desert: The Loss of Local News.* Chapel Hill, NC: University of North Carolina.

Althaus, S. L., Cizmar, A. M., and Gimpel, J. G. (2009) Media supply, audience demand, and the geography of news consumption in the United States. *Political Communication,* 26(3), 249–277.

Alvarez, R. M. and Brehm, J. (2002) *Hard Choices, Easy Answers: Values, Information and American Public Opinion.* Princeton, NJ: Princeton University Press.

Anderson, C. W. (2013) *Rebuilding the News: Metropolitan Journalism in the Digital Age.* Philadelphia, PA: Temple University Press.

Badger, E. Quealy, K., and Katz, J. (2021) Close-up picture of the partisan segregation in the U.S. *New York Times,* April 20, A18–19.

Bakhtin, M. M. (1981) *The Dialogic Imagination: Four Essays by M.M. Bakhtin.* Translated by C. Emerson and M. Holquist. Austin: University of Texas Press.

Barrett, R. (2019) As dairy crisis crushes farmers, Wisconsin's rural identity in jeopardy, *Milwaukee Journal Sentinel,* January 11.

Barthel, M. (2019) Newspapers fact sheet. Washington, DC: Pew Research Center.

Benkler, Y., Faris, R., and Roberts, H. (2018) *Network Propaganda: Manipulation, Disinformation, and Radicalization in American Politics.* New York: Oxford University Press.

Bennett, W. L. (2011) *News: The Politics of Illusion.* 9th edition. Boston, MA: Pearson.

Castells, M. (2007) Communication, power and counter-power in the network society. *International Journal of Communication,* 1(1), 29.

Castells, M. (2010) *The Rise of the Network Society: The Information Age: Economy, Society, and Culture Volume I.* 2nd edition with a new preface. Chichester, UK; Malden, MA: Wiley-Blackwell.

Centola, D. (2015) The social origins of networks and diffusion. *American Journal of Sociology,* 120(5), 1295–1338.

Chadwick, A. (2017) *The Hybrid Media System: Politics and Power.* New York: Oxford University Press.

Chen, J. and Rodden, J. (2013) Unintentional gerrymandering: Political geography and electoral bias in legislatures. *Quarterly Journal of Political Science,* 8(3), 239–269.

Couldry, N. and Hepp, A. (2016) *The Mediated Construction of Reality.* Cambridge, UK; Malden, MA: Polity.

Cramer, K. J. (2004) *Talking about Politics: Informal Groups and Social Identity in American Life.* Chicago, IL: University of Chicago Press.

Cramer, K. J. (2007) *Talking about Race: Community Dialogues and the Politics of Difference.* Chicago, IL: University of Chicago Press.

Cramer, K. J. (2016) *The Politics of Resentment: Rural Consciousness in Wisconsin and the Rise of Scott Walker.* Chicago, IL: University of Chicago Press.

Cramer, K. J. (forthcoming) Deflecting from racism: Local talk radio conversation about George Floyd, in Lupu, N. and Pontusson, J. (eds.) *Unequal Democracies: Public Policy, Responsiveness, and Redistribution in an Era of Rising Economic Inequality.*

Daley, D. (2016) *Ratf**ked: The True Story behind the Secret Plan to Steal America's Democracy.* New York: Liveright.

Darmstra, A., Jacobs, L., Boukes, M., and Vliegenthart, R. (2021) The impact of immigration news on anti-immigrant party support: Unpacking agenda-setting and issue ownership effects over time. *Journal of Elections, Public Opinion and Parties*, 31(1), 97–118.

De Vreese, C. H., Boukes, M., Schuck, A., et al. (2017) Linking survey and media content data: Opportunities, considerations, and pitfalls. *Communication Methods and Measures*, 11(4), 221–244.

Delli Carpini, M. X. (1996) *What Americans Know about Politics and Why It Matters.* New Haven, CT: Yale University Press.

Dempsey, S., Suk, J., Cramer, K. J., et al. (2021) Understanding Trump supporters' news use: Beyond the Fox News bubble. *The Forum*, 18(3), 319–346. https://doi.org/10.1515/for-2020-2012.

Dresser, L. and Rogers, J. (2019) *The State of Working Wisconsin 2019: Facts and Figures.* Madison: University of Wisconsin–Madison.

Edgerly, S. (2015) Red media, blue media, and purple media: News repertoires in the colorful media landscape. *Journal of Broadcasting & Electronic Media*, 59(1), 1–21.

Ellis, C. and Stimson, J. A. (2012) *Ideology in America.* New York: Cambridge University Press.

Enders, C. K. and Tofighi, D. (2007) Centering predictor variables in cross-sectional multilevel models: A new look at an old issue. *Psychological Methods*, 12(2), 121.

Fagan, E. J. (2021) Issue ownership and the priorities of party elites in the United States, 2004–2016. *Party Politics*, 27(1), 149–160.

Friedland, L. A. (2001) Communication, community, and democracy: Toward a theory of the communicatively integrated community. *Communication Research*, 28(4), 358–391.

Friedland, L. A. (2014) Civic communication in a networked society: Seattle's emergent ecology, in Girouard, J. and Sirianni, C. (eds.) *Varieties of Civic Innovation: Deliberative, Collaborative, Network, and Narrative Approaches*. Nashville, TN: Vanderbilt University Press, pp.92–126.

Friedland, L. A. (2016) Networks in place. *American Behavioral Scientist*, 60 (1), 24–42.

Friedland, L. (2020) Wisconsin: Laboratory of oligarchy, in Goldberg, C. A. (ed.) *Education for Democracy: Renewing the Wisconsin Idea*. Madison: University of Wisconsin Press, pp. 224–254.

Gilbert, C. (2018) Wisconsin gerrymandering: Data shows stark impact of redistricting. *Milwaukee Journal Sentinel*, December 6. www.jsonline.com /story/news/blogs/wisconsin-voter/2018/12/06/wisconsin-gerrymandering-data-shows-stark-impact-redistricting/2219092002/.

Gilbert, C. (2020) Wisconsin election results: Democrats assemble a winning map. *Milwaukee Journal Sentinel*, April 14. www.jsonline.com/story/news/ politics/analysis/2020/04/14/wisconsin-election-results-democrats-assemble -winning-map/2988171001/.

Gimpel, J. (2019) From wedge issue to partisan divide: The development of immigration policy opinion after 2016. *The Forum*, 17(3), 467–486.

Gruszczynski, M. and Wagner, M. W. (2017) Information flow in the 21st century: The dynamics of agenda-uptake. *Mass Communication and Society*, 20(3), 378–402.

Guess, A., Lyons, B., Nyhan, B., and Reifler, J. (2018) *Avoiding the Echo Chamber about Echo Chambers: Why Selective Exposure to Like-Minded Political News Is Less Prevalent Than You Think*. Miami, FL: Knight Foundation.

Habermas, J. (1987) *The Theory of Communicative Action, Volume 2: Lifeworld and System: A Critique of Functionalist Reason* (T. McCarthy, trans.). Boston, MA: Beacon Press.

Hall, D. J. and Vetterkind, R. (2017) How undocumented immigrants became the backbone of dairies –And how to keep the milk flowing in America's Dairyland. *Wisconsin Center for Investigative Journalism*, October 6. https:// bit.ly/3GUCXk3.

Hampton, K. (2016) Persistent and pervasive community: New communication technologies and the future of community. *American Behavioral Scientist*, 60 (1), 101–124.

Hayes, D. and Lawless, J. L. (2017) The decline of local news and its effects: New evidence from longitudinal data. *The Journal of Politics*, 80(1), 332–336.

Hertel-Fernandez, A. (2019. *State Capture: How Conservative Activists, Big Businesses, and Wealthy Donors Reshaped the American States – and the Nation*. New York and London: Oxford University Press.

Hochschild, A. R. (2016) *Strangers in Their Own Land: Anger and Mourning on the American Right*. New York: The New Press.

Hopkins, D. (2018) *The Increasingly United States*. Chicago, IL: University of Chicago Press.

Horwitz, R. B. (2013) *America's Right: Anti-Establishment Conservatism from Goldwater to the Tea Party*. Hoboken, NJ: John Wiley & Sons.

Huckfeldt, R. R. and Sprague, J. (1995) *Citizens, Politics and Social Communication: Information and Influence in an Election Campaign*. New York: Cambridge University Press.

Jamieson, K. H. and Cappella, J. N. (2008) *Echo Chamber: Rush Limbaugh and the Conservative Media Establishment*. New York: Oxford University Press.

Jungherr, A., Posegga, O., and An, J. (2019) Discursive power in contemporary media systems: A comparative framework. *The International Journal of Press/Politics*, 24(4), 404–425.

Jungherr, A., Rivero, G., and Gayo-Avello, D. (2020) *Retooling Politics: How Digital Media Are Shaping Democracy*. New York: Cambridge University Press.

Kaniss, P. (1991) *Making Local News*. Chicago, IL: University of Chicago Press.

Katz, E. and Lazarsfeld, P. F. (1955) *Personal Influence: The Part Played by People in the Flow Of Mass Communications*. New York: The Free Press.

Kaufman, D. (2018) *The Fall of Wisconsin: The Conservative Conquest of a Progressive Bastion and the Future of American Politics*. New York: W. W. Norton & Company.

Kettl, D. F. (2020) *The Divided States of America: Why Federalism Doesn't Work*. Princeton, NJ: Princeton University Press.

Kim, N., Konieczna, M., Yoon, H. Y., and Friedland, L. A. (2016) Sustainability factors of emergent civic news websites: A qualitative comparative analysis approach. *Journalism & Mass Communication Quarterly*, 93(4), 750–769.

Konieczna, M. (2018) *Journalism without Profit: Making News When the Market Fails*. New York: Oxford University Press.

Krasno, J., Magleby, D. B., McDonald, M. D., Donahue, S., and Best, R. E. (2019) Can gerrymanders be detected? An examination of Wisconsin's state assembly. *American Politics Research*, 47(5), 1162–1201.

Levendusky, M. S. (2021) How does local TV news change viewers' attitudes? The case of Sinclair Broadcasting. *Political Communication.* https://doi.org /10.1080/10584609.2021.1901807.

Martin, G. J. and McCrain, J. (2019) Local news and national politics. *American Political Science Review,* 113(2), 372–384.

Mason, L. (2018). *Uncivil Agreement.* Chicago, IL and London: University of Chicago Press.

Mason, L., Wronski, J., and Kane, J. V. (2021) Activating animus: The uniquely social roots of trump support. *American Political Science Review,* 115(4), 1508–1516.

Matsaganis, M. D., Katz, V. S., and Ball-Rokeach, S. J. (2010) *Understanding Ethnic Media: Producers, Consumers, and Societies.* Los Angeles, CA: Sage Publications.

McGregor, S. C. (2019) Social media as public opinion: How journalists use social media to represent public opinion. *Journalism* 20(8), 1070–1086.

McGregor S. C. and Molyneux L. (2020) Twitter's influence on news judgment: An experiment among journalists. *Journalism* 21(5), 597–613.

McLeod, D. M. and Shah, D. V. (2015) *News Frames and National Security.* New York: Cambridge University Press.

McPherson, M., Smith-Lovin, L., and Cook, J. M. (2001) Birds of a feather: Homophily in social networks. *Annual Review of Sociology,* 27, 415–444.

Mellon, J. and Prosser, C. (2017) Twitter and Facebook are not representative of the general population: Political attitudes and demographics of British social media users. *Research & Politics,* 4(3), 2053168017720008. https://doi.org /10.1177/2053168017720008.

Mitchell, A. and Matsa, K. E. (2019) For local news, Americans embrace digital but still want strong community connection. Pew Research Center, March 26.

Mitchell, M. D., Farren, M. D., Horpedahl, J., and Gonzalez, O. (2020) The economics of a targeted economic development subsidy. *Mercatus Center Research Paper.* www.mercatus.org/system/files/mitchell-targeted-development-mercatus-special-study-v3.pdf.

Nakagawa, S., Johnson, P. C., and Schielzeth, H. (2017) The coefficient of determination R2 and intra-class correlation coefficient from generalized linear mixed-effects models revisited and expanded. *Journal of the Royal Society Interface,* 14(134), 1–11.

Napoli, P. M. (2018) *Assessing Local Journalism: News Deserts, Journalism Divides, and the Determinants of the Robustness of Local News.* Durham, NC: Sanford School for Public Policy, Duke University.

National Association of Manufacturers (n.d.) 2019Wisconsin manufacturing facts. www.nam.org/state-manufacturing-data/2019-wisconsin-manufacturing-facts/.

Neuman, W. R., Guggenheim, L., Jang, S. M., and Bae, S. Y. (2014) The dynamics of public attention: Agenda-setting theory meets big data, *Journal of Communication*, 64(2), 193–214.

Nielsen, R. K. (2015) The Uncertain Future of Local Journalism, in Nielsen, R. K. (ed.) *Local Journalism: The Decline of Newspapers and the Rise of Digital Media*. London: I.B. Tauris, pp. 1–25.

Ognyanova, K. (2019) The social context of media trust: A network influence model. *Journal of Communication*, 69(5), 41.

Page, S. (2010) *Diversity and Complexity*. Princeton, NJ: Princeton University Press.

Perez, M. (2019) Wisconsin's dairy industry would collapse without the work of Latino immigrants – many of them undocumented. *Milwaukee Journal Sentinel*, November 12. https://bit.ly/3nR9yOP.

Peters, A. and Fisher, P. (2004) The failures of economic development incentives. *Journal of the American Planning Association*, 70(1), 27–37.

Polletta, F. and Callahan, J. (2017) Deep stories, nostalgia narratives, and fake news: Storytelling in the Trump era. *American Journal of Cultural Sociology*, 5(3), 392–408.

Petrocik, J. R. (1996) Issue ownership in presidential elections, with a 1980 case study. *American Journal of Political Science*, 40(3), 825–850.

Posegga, O. and Jungherr, A. (2019) Characterizing political talk on Twitter: A comparison between public agenda, media agendas, and the Twitter agenda with regard to topics and dynamics. *Proceedings of the 52nd Hawaii International Conference on System Sciences*, 2590–2599.

Prais, S. J. and Winsten, C. B. (1954) Trend estimators and serial correlation. Cowles Commission Discussion Paper, 383, 1–26.

Prior, M. (2007) *Post-Broadcast Democracy: How Media Choice Increases Inequality in Political Involvement and Polarizes Elections*. New York: Cambridge University Press.

Robinson, S. (2017) *Networked News, Racial Divides: How Power and Privilege Shape Public Discourse in Progressive Communities*. Cambridge: Cambridge University Press.

Rodden, J. (2019) *Why Cities Lose: The Deep Roots of the Urban–Rural Political Divide*. New York: Basic Books.

Rodrik, D. (2016) Premature deindustrialization. *Journal of Economic Growth*, 21(1), 1–33.

Schutz, A. and Luckmann, T. (1973) *The Structures of the Life-world*. Evanston, IL: Northwestern University Press.

Shah, D. V., McLeod, J. M., and Yoon, S. H. (2001) Communication, context, and community: An exploration of print, broadcast, and internet influences. *Communication Research*, 28(4), 464–506.

Shah, D. V., Watts, M. D., Domke, D., and Fan, D. P. (2002). News framing and cueing of issue regimes: Explaining Clinton's public approval in spite of scandal. *Public Opinion Quarterly*, 66(3), 339–370.

Shah, D. V., Cho, J., Eveland Jr., W. P., and Kwak, N. (2005) Information and expression in a digital age: Modeling internet effects on civic participation. *Communication Research*, 32(5), 531–565.

Shah, D. V., Cappella, J. N., and Neuman, W. R. (2015) Big data, digital media, and computational social science: Possibilities and perils. *The ANNALS of the American Academy of Political and Social Science*, 659(1), 6–13.

Shah, D. V., McLeod, D. M., Rojas, H., et al. (2017) Revising the communication mediation model for a new political communication ecology. *Human Communication Research*, 43(4), 491–504.

Shearer, E. and Mitchell, A. (2021) News use across social media platforms in 2020. Pew Research Center, January 12.

Skocpol, T. and Williamson, V. (2012) *The Tea Party and the Remaking of Republican Conservatism*. New York and London: Oxford University Press.

Solt, F. (2008) Economic inequality and democratic political engagement. *American Journal of Political Science*, 52(1), 48–60

Spicuzza, M. and Marley, P. (2019) Liberal groups take cue from the right with new websites in Wisconsin, *Milwaukee Journal Sentinel*, August 23.

Stein, J. and Marley, P. (2013) *More Than They Bargained for: Scott Walker, Unions and the Fight for Wisconsin*. Madison: University of Wisconsin Press.

Strauss, C. (2012) *Making Sense of Public Opinion: American Discourses about Immigration and Social Programs*. New York: Cambridge University Press.

Suk, J., Dhah, D. V., Wells, C., et al. (2020) Do improving conditions harden partisan preferences? Lived experiences, imagined communities, and polarized Evaluations. *International Journal of Public Opinion Research*, 32(4), 750–768.

Tahk, A. M. (2015) A continuous-time, latent-variable model of time series data. *Political Analysis*, 23(2), 278–298.

Thorson, K. and Wells, C. (2015) Curated flows: A framework for mapping media exposure in the digital age. *Communication Theory*, 26(3), 309–328.

Thorson, K., Medeiros, M., Cotter, K., et al. (2020) Platform civics: Facebook in the local information infrastructure. *Digital Journalism*, 8(10), 1231–1257.

Usher, N. (2017) Venture-backed news startups and the field of journalism: Challenges, changes, and consistencies. *Digital Journalism*, 5(9), 1116–1133.

Usher, N. (2019) Putting "place" in the center of journalism research: A way forward to understand challenges to trust and knowledge in news. *Journalism & Communication Monographs*, 21(2), 84–146.

Vargo, C. and Guo, L. (2017) Networks, big data, and intermedia agenda setting: An analysis of traditional, partisan, and emerging online U.S. news. *Journalism & Mass Communication Quarterly*, 94(4), 1031–1055.

Vavreck, L. (2009) *The Message Matters: The Economy and Presidential Campaigns*. Princeton, NJ: Princeton University Press.

Vogelsang, T. J. (1998) Trend function hypothesis testing in the presence of serial correlation. *Econometrica*, 66(1), 123–148.

Wagner, M. W. and Gruszczynski, M. (2016) When framing matters: How partisan and journalistic frames affect individual opinions and party identification. *Journalism & Communication Monographs*, 18(1), 5–48.

Wagner, M. W., Wells, C., Friedland, L. A., Cramer, K. J., and Shah, D. V. (2014) Cultural worldviews and contentious politics: Evaluative asymmetry in high-information environments. *The Good Society*, 23(2), 126–144.

Walter, D. and Ophir, Y. (2019) News frame analysis: An inductive mixed-method computational approach. *Communication Methods and Measures*, 13(4), 248–266.

Wells, C., Shah, D. V., Pevehouse, J. C., et al. (2016) How trump drove coverage to the nomination: Hybrid media campaigning. *Political Communication*, 33 (4), 669–676.

Wells, C., Cramer, K. J., Wagner, M. W., et al. (2017). When we stop talking politics: The maintenance and closing of conversation in contentious times. *Journal of Communication*, 67(1), 131–157.

Wells, C., Shah, D. V., Pevehouse, J. C., et al.(2019). The temporal turn in communication research: Time series analyses using computational approaches. *International Journal of Communication*, 13, 4021–4043.

Wells, C., Friedland, L. A., Hughes, C., et al. (2021) News media use, talk networks, and anti-elitism across geographic location: Evidence from Wisconsin. *The International Journal of Press/Politics*, 26(2), 438–463.

Williams, B. and Delli Carpini, M. (2011) *After Broadcast News: Media Regimes, Democracy, and the New Information Environment*. New York: Cambridge University Press.

Witkovsky, B. (2021) National politics, local fissures: A closer look at the rural–urban divide. Annual Meeting of the American Sociological Association, November 17–20, 2021, Montreal, CA.

Wojcieszak, M. and Garrett, R. K. (2018) Social identity, selective exposure, and affective polarization: How priming national identity shapes attitudes toward immigrants via news selection. *Human Communication Research*, 44 (3), 247–273.

Zaller, J. (1992) *The Nature and Origins of Mass Opinion*. Cambridge and New York: Cambridge University Press.

Interviews Cited

Peter Fox, newspaper executive, retired, 2020.
Dean Kallenbach, Wisconsin Public Radio, retired, 2020.
Brian Reisinger, political consultant, 2017.
Charlie Sykes, former talk show host, 2017.

Acknowledgments

We applied much of what we learned from our colleagues across the globe at two conferences we hosted while working on the project. We are grateful to the presenters at our "Communication, Populism and the Crisis of Democracy" conference in 2018 and our "Fractured Democracy" conference in 2019: Julia Azari, Lance Bennett, Sheri Berman, Sven Engesser, Frank Esser, Richard Fletcher, Sandra González-Bailón, Lei Guo, Andreas Jungherr, Mike Kearney, Karolina Koc-Michalska, Daniel Kreiss, Alice Marwick, Lilliana Mason, Jörg Matthes, Shannon McGregor, Pippa Norris, Deb Roy, Claudia Strauss, Talia Stroud, and Silvio Waisbord.

We are thankful for our former students, who have worked on elements of the larger project, German Alvarez, Leticia Bode, Stephanie Edgerly, Alex Hanna, and Meredith Metzler, and our colleagues at the University of Wisconsin with whom we have shared ideas and insights, Douglas McLeod, Hernando Rojas, Hemant Shah, Barry Burden, Nils Ringe, and Elizabeth Covington as well as Carmen Sirianni of Brandeis.

We are indebted to Charles Franklin, both for sharing Marquette Law School Poll data with us and for continuing to work with us on matters related to survey research. We also thank Karl Rohe and Bill Sethares, our co-investigators on a number of the grants that support this work. We thank Malia Jones and Rozalynn Klaas of the UW Applied Population Lab for essential advice in building our statewide database. Without Rowan Calyx and Jenni Hart in the SJMC main office, we could not have written this Element.

We are so proud of our current and recent students who contributed directly to this Element: Aman Abhishek, Monica Sansonetti Busch, Sadie Dempsey, Zening Duan, Jordan Foley, Ceri Hughes, Xiaoya Jiang, Jianing Li, Josephine Lukito, Meredith Metzler, Catherine Daily Pickart, Ruixue Lian, Jiyoun Suk, Zhongkai Sun, Yiming Wang, Ellie Yang, and Yini Zhang.

Our superb editor, Heath Sledge greatly improved the manuscript and made the collaborative writing process much better. We thank our series editor, Stuart Soroka and two anonymous reviewers for extensive comments that sharpened our argument considerably.

Support for this research was provided by the John S. and James L. Knight Foundation with thanks to John Sands and Sam Gill, the University of Wisconsin - Madison Office of the Vice Chancellor for Research and Graduate Education. We were also supported by funding from the Wisconsin Alumni Research Foundation, the Center for European Studies at UW-Madison, the Jean Monnet European Centre of Excellence, the William + Flora Hewlett Foundation, the UW- Madison Fall Competition, The Greater Milwaukee Foundation, Carnegie Corporation of New York, the Robert F. and Jean E. Holtz Center, Love Wisconsin, and endowments to the University of Wisconsin-Madison.

Finally, all of us thank our families without whose tolerance, patience (and occasional criticism) we would not have been able to complete this project.

Cambridge Elements ≡

Politics and Communication

Stuart Soroka

University of California

Stuart Soroka is a Professor in the Department of Communication at the University of California, Los Angeles, and Adjunct Research Professor at the Center for Political Studies at the Institute for Social Research, University of Michigan. His research focuses on political communication, political psychology, and the relationships between public policy, public opinion, and mass media. His books with Cambridge University Press include *The Increasing Viability of Good News* (2021, with Yanna Krupnikov), *Negativity in Democratic Politics* (2014), *Information and Democracy* (forthcoming, with Christopher Wlezien) and *Degrees of Democracy* (2010, with Christopher Wlezien).

About the series

Cambridge Elements in Politics and Communication publishes research focused on the intersection of media, technology, and politics. The series emphasizes forward-looking reviews of the field, path-breaking theoretical and methodological innovations, and the timely application of social-scientific theory and methods to current developments in politics and communication around the world.

Cambridge Elements ☰

Politics and Communication

Printed in the United States
by Baker & Taylor Publisher Services